PARENT DELETED

The Urbana Free Library

To renew: call **217-367-4057**
or go to **urbanafreelibrary.org**
and select **My Account**

D1114345

PARENT DELETED

A Mother's Fight For
Her Right to Parent

MICHELLE DARNÉ

SHE WRITES PRESS

Published 2017
Printed in the United States of America
ISBN: 978-1-63152-282-6 pbk
ISBN: 978-1-63152-283-3 ebk
Library of Congress Control Number: 2017937341

Interior design by Tabitha Lahr

For information, address:
She Writes Press
1563 Solano Ave #546
Berkeley, CA 94707

She Writes Press is a division of SparkPoint Studio, LLC.

This book is dedicated to my daughters.

To my mother, for without you and your strength, your belief in me, and your love for me, this book would not have been possible.

And to my father. You are kind and proud—the hardest-working person I know, and someone who would give a stranger his last five dollars and the shirt off his back. My fight comes from you; you have taught me to never give up, to be proud of my heritage, and to wake up with a smile because every day is a day to begin again.

PREFACE

CONTEXT: the set of circumstances or facts that surround a particular event or situation.

Parental alienation is when a parent tries to damage or destroy a relationship between his or her child(ren) and the other parent. Parental alienation affects the lives of more than 22 million parents in the US alone (Harman, Leder-Elder & Biringen, 2016).

Many targeted parents are silent about their experience because others do not often believe them ("they must be doing something to deserve it"), they fear retaliation from the other parent, they are concerned about the impact it may have on their child(ren), or they end up blaming themselves for the other parent's behaviors. I commend Darné for her bravery in sharing her story so that others can learn they are not alone.

Parental alienation does not discriminate; it affects people of all nationalities and sociodemographic groups, and it does not just affect parents—any parental figure in a child's life (e.g., a grandparent) can be susceptible. To date, researchers know very little about how this problem affects parents from same-sex couples, which is one of the many reasons Darné's story is so important. With same-sex marriage being legalized across many countries in the world, it is important to understand how divorce and separation in these relationships is similar to and varies from "traditional" heterosexual relationships where children are involved at the time of dissolution.

Parental-alienating behaviors and their impact on same-sex parents do not vary considerably from those experienced by other targets of alienation; many of these parents struggle with feelings of depression, anxiety, post-traumatic stress disorder, and extreme ambiguous loss and disenfranchised grief. But a same-sex parent may not have the same rights to her children as many alienated parents do, due to her not being their biological parent.

Darné's story resembles those of many stepparents and adoptive parents I have interviewed in my research; she, however, has had to face additional stigma and discrimination in family court due to her being from a same-sex relationship. Family law and courts are slow to adjust to societal changes in family structures, and, unfortunately, this leaves many individuals, like Darné, vulnerable to the tactics of parents who are not afraid to use the system to their advantage. Societal norms about gender and parenting (e.g., who makes the "better" parent), reflected in family court laws and their application, help to sanction the abusive behaviors of parents who alienate their children from other loving adults in their lives (Harman & Biringen, 2016).

Despite her struggles, Darné's story also carries a message of hope. Her candor resonates with the reader and leads to a deep understanding of her experience. She paves the way for others to also speak their truths—truths that will cast light on the shadows into which they have been thrown and that will allow us as a society to stop unknowingly sanctioning these behaviors. With this book, Darné has given us a real gift—a gift that promotes understanding and enables empathy, both prerequisites for being able to work collaboratively toward solutions to this problem, a problem that needs to end for sake of our children and those who love them.

—Jennifer J. Harman, PhD, coauthor of *Parents Acting Badly: How Institutions and Societies Promote the Alienation of Children from their Loving Families* (2016) and Associate Professor of Psychology at Colorado State University

AUTHOR'S NOTE

The impetus for this book wasn't my desire to tell my story. In fact, I prayed that I would never have to write it. For five long years, riven, I grappled with the idea. I would have preferred not to make my life and the lives of my children any more public than they have already been.

Neither it is my intent to shock, even though some of the details of my story may seem graphic and dismay some readers. I hope the inclusion of those details will serve the higher purpose of depicting the truth of the devastation that unfolds when bias and false allegations are allowed to preside in society and the courtroom.

This is my story, told from my vantage point.

The details are drawn from my memory, aided by a mound of e-mails, court records, and transcripts from court proceedings and testimony, as well as recollections of others who witnessed the events depicted in this book. Wherever possible, as in the case of court records and written communication, exact quotes have been preserved and repeated. In cases of past exchanges, casual conversations, mediation sessions where no transcript was produced, and other cases where I have only my memory to rely on, I have endeavored to preserve the meanings of those exchanges to the best of my recollection, and also to relate the words as accurately as possible.

To protect their privacy, the names of all children mentioned in this book, and of the adults in their lives, as well as the names of my staff and attorneys, have been changed.

Some may disagree with the opinions expressed here, and others may be angry that I have written this book. However, I had to do it. Even if only one person benefits from reading my story, this book will have fulfilled its aim. *Parent Deleted* aims for resolution, not retaliation.

CHAPTER 1:
LOVE CHILD

AUDACITY: boldness or daring, especially with confident or arrogant disregard for personal safety, conventional thought, or other restrictions.

"You know, you can become anything you want."

My first memory is from when I was barely three. My mother was rocking me, cradling me in her arms—something she had always done and would continue to do.

As was its prerogative, her voice had taken charge; neither my temper nor my scrappy little body could resist her affections.

"You just have to believe."

In the years to come, her sweet scent would draw my thoughts home from the schoolyard, from the ball fields, from the dramas of childhood.

"You can end up anywhere in the world you wish."

Lush, lyrical, and a little raspy, my mother's voice engulfed me, disarming my anger and soothing my aches without fail.

It would take years for me to realize just how audacious

this was of my mother, a small Puerto Rican woman raised in Hawaii before being married off at thirteen to an abusive man. She left him after having his three children, the oldest only fourteen years my mother's junior, to carve—or claw, if need be—a better path for herself and her children.

When it came to children, my mother topped out at eleven: she had six by two husbands, and another four came with her life's mate, my father. They refer to me as the "love child," number eleven—my lucky number.

My mother's tenacity for a better life, however unimaginable, linked thousands of children to their future as she drove their school bus, and it elevated the aspirations of countless more before she retired as a highly respected driver trainer and union representative. Never mind that she never had the opportunity to get past eighth grade.

"If you can dream it, you can do it."

And did I ever dream.

———

"Uh-oh . . ."

"That's it, Darné. You've struck out."

"Please, Mr. Christianson . . . Please. I really don't want to get in trouble."

"I did warn you, didn't I?"

"Please, Mr. Christianson. Anything you want. Surely there is something I can do for you."

And there I was, negotiating my way out of trouble. While putting out my cigarette, which I was smoking behind the school gym when, you guessed it, I was supposed to be in class. This was the third time Mr. Christianson had caught me. That week. So there was no faking my motivation for timely attendance of my tenth-grade classes.

"Okay, so this is how we are going to play it," he said.

"Either you go straight to the principal's office, or you join my journalism class. We need help with the newspaper and the yearbook. Your choice, Darné."

Great, I thought. *I've officially become a geek.*

And that was how I got pushed into a career in communications.

I might have been meant for it: I'm a Gemini (a sign known for communication ability) who was born into an oversized Puerto Rican household where advocating for oneself was a condition of survival. I talked at seven months of age. Given that I had already been walking for a month by that point (a lot to do, so little time!), I did the advocating while dashing underneath tabletops upright. I never topped five foot one, so some might say I got used to the convenience.

The first journalism class I attended, I just listened. In addition to the class, the newspaper folk met after school a couple of times a week. I found myself getting drawn in, speaking up, getting involved. Within a week, I was made the advertising manager, and within two weeks I had my own desk—with a phone, of course—set up at school, and had hired an assistant (who had been my best friend since we were five).

By this point in my life, I had discovered how to use my gifts in negotiating my own life. Despite struggling with subjects that required studying, I sailed through intermediate school (in California, that was seventh and eighth grades) on my own terms because I was creating, choreographing, and directing school productions that were selling out and making money for the school.

Outside of school, I started working. Initially, I did odd jobs like painting houses. Between saving most of what I made and automatically being a member of the Mount Diablo Credit Union (my mother is member #67 to this day), by fifteen I was able to buy my first car, even though I could not drive a stick and would not have been legally allowed to even if I could. My dad had to drive it home from the seller on my behalf. My payment was a sweet $62.50 per month.

One of my brothers was a big wheel at Albertsons, the grocery store. However, he was resistant to my arguments as to why he should help me get a job there. So when I was fifteen and a half, before it was legal for anybody to hire me, I went straight to the store management and hounded them for weeks. I had a job as a courtesy clerk, aka grocery bagger, the moment I turned sixteen—with benefits, mind you.

At school, that meant I was getting outside work experience, or OWE, and that earned me school credit. So my formal education shrank to fit between 8:00 a.m. and noon, the rest liberated for money making—and soccer, as I had been playing club ball with a traveling team since I was eight. Club, or league sport, was what kids turned to if they wanted more, and could achieve more, than school sport programs had to offer. It was perfect for me.

I was also attending evening school, as I was following my calling, as I saw it at the time, by taking classes in fire science in order to become a firefighter.

There was, however, one more thing going on in my life, and it wasn't as productive as the others—at least, not personally. I had tried cocaine when I was fourteen, and by sixteen I knew I liked it. Within another year, I also knew that I was really good at selling it, and that it made me much better money than any legal job I could possibly have.

As a result, by the time Mr. Christianson held that power trip over me, I was financially independent, thoroughly self-aware, and a social renegade—a young woman who now had a media pass to show to all those "narcs" (my term for the aging women who patrolled our closed campus to ensure we did not escape, not even in our minds). Probably once truly kind, these narcs had since succumbed to frustration with everything under the age of sixteen, and went truly CDC (Centers for Disease Control) over somebody like me.

———

That was the year I got hurt out of my future. Soccer was my first love. Fast. Combustive. Mutual. On the field, my heart sang, and I gave myself fully to it.

Tough, single-minded, and relentless, I was good at hiding an ankle injury that had plagued me on and off during the regular season. I lied to my mother. Out of 6,500 talented soccer teens, I was chosen to represent the United States at the next world games in Europe. Society had not yet evolved to the level of professional women's soccer, so I made it as far as I could go.

"The eye of the tiger," as my father would say, could not conceal that I was sometimes unable to get my cleats on because my ankle was too swollen. Finally, I conceded. My doctor x-rayed it, and there it was: a hairline fracture that sidelined me, put me in a cast and on crutches, and broke my heart.

I did not have to step off the team. I could have still gone to Europe. But my mother said what I did not want to hear: "You know, there is another kid within that 6,500 that could actually play."

Doing the right thing is rarely easy, especially at sixteen. But I somberly stepped aside. Some other girl's future took place while I stayed home and filled my free time, and my hollow heart, with cocaine.

As a result, by eighteen my drug addiction was controlling my life. Not that I knew it. I was dealing and making all sorts of cash. I always kept a couple grand in my pocket, deposited a non-conspicuous amount into my bank account every now and again, and partied on the rest.

I turned eighteen and graduated from high school on the same day. The very next day, I moved out of home and into my own apartment in a maneuver that addicts call the "geographical cure." Namely, I requested a transfer with Albertson's from Pleasant Hill to Citrus Heights, two hours away from the Bay Area. The salary no longer motivated me, but the benefits and vast client base did—and I also thought that if I moved, got away from my routine, I could get a grip on my addition.

Needless to say, it don't work that way. In fact, after moving I was high most of the time, business was booming, and I was coming to San Francisco weekly to pick up a new load. Eventually, I had to quit Albertsons because I partied too much and did not show up to work enough.

CDF, the California Department of Forestry, hired new firefighters once a year, and only after rigorous mental and physical testing. As such, I had to wait some six months after graduation to apply, during which time I moved back to the Bay Area. For the year I was undergoing my rigorous training, I pushed the drugs out and focused, and I wound up setting the record for the highest score on the oral exam while exceeding all expectations of my physical ability. These accomplishments gave me the right to choose any location for my first placement. I could have started a new life in one of the many gorgeous towns along California's coast. I, however, made a business decision as a dealer: I selected the fire station ten minutes from my home.

At 105 pounds, I was the smallest and scrappiest firefighter in my unit, and the only girl. Over the following two and a half years, I experienced it all. I descended into raging fires off helicopters, saved wildlife and stranded people alike, ran for my life while carrying my body weight in gear, baked alive in fire bags, and hacked up soot for days after a major blaze.

My schedule was sweet: three days on, four off. The latter meant lots of time for money making. I grew my occasional custom-painting gigs into a sought-after custom-painting business, working on high-profile restaurants, gyms, luxury homes, and more. And my dealing business was flourishing. It was all fun; in fact, parties didn't take off until I arrived. Dealing drugs is quite the ego booster. My clients were upstanding citizens: doctors, lawyers, and their beautiful, ambitious friends. I was on top of the world, pulling in thousands of dollars per week. And my addiction was not only back but stronger than ever.

One day, I was summoned in during my off time. The fire department has the right, called "c-manning power," to call in all firefighters, on- and off-duty, during emergencies. That day, I put a fellow firefighter in danger because I was hungover, and it weighed heavily on me. And since I didn't turn up my normal chipper, swift self—amazing how well people know you when you nearly live together—my chief came to check on me at my home the following day. Not a good sign when your chief shows up on your doorstep.

I stepped outside. It was late morning, and the sun was almost directly above us. After a few moments of silence, Chief confirmed his reason for being there.

"I am worried about you, M." I could see the look of concern in his eyes. He didn't know what exactly I was on, but he clearly knew I was on something.

"Not sure you know this, but they will start doing random drug tests any day now," he continued.

No, I didn't know, and this wasn't a change I could take lightly.

"I hope you will choose to stay."

It was his kind eyes and the unspoken words that got me. Much can be said in silence. I could have gotten help, all paid for through our generous benefits. All I had to do was be honest, humble. But the truth is, I didn't want to get sober. So I resigned, in part because I was scared of risking more lives—my soul must have intervened, even though at the time, I didn't know I had one—and also because I really didn't want to be dismissed for misconduct.

Over the months that ensued, I lived every inch of the downward spiral. I was in drug oblivion, consuming a gram and a half of cocaine a day and letting everything else fall by the wayside. It was no longer fun, because I had gotten to a point where I had to sell in order to fund my addiction. My mother stopped talking to me and insisted that all my siblings follow suit. She did, however, show up to get me out of jail when I got picked up for driving under the influence. That night I promised her I would stop drinking and drugging. But I lied. In another six months, I was broke and hollow, slain and treading my rock bottom. Oh, and all those so-called friends? They were nowhere to be found. I was twenty-two years old, and I was sure that my life was over.

One night, soaking wet from head to toe after getting caught in a torrential downpour in Vallejo, California, I stumbled into a pay phone booth and called my sister collect, begging her to come get me. To this day, I have no idea how she found me, as I was so high I didn't know where I was. She helped me get into a program, and I've never had a line since—or a drink, because I had no interest in finding out exactly what influence alcohol had on my drug addiction. That was the darkest chapter of my life. It hurts to think, let alone write, about it. But my sobriety is one of only two achievements I am truly proud of. And the second was yet to occur.

———

At twenty-three, when most people are just starting their partying days, my own had come to an end. Clean and sober and starting my life over, I took a job with the *Contra Costa Times,* loading newspapers into trucks—my first paid gig in the industry. Once again, I was the only girl on the seventeen-person crew. And once again, I quickly started driving the team, making mundane work fun, creating competition through games that pushed me and the guys to set goals and exceed our best.

Unbeknownst to me, during one of these work sessions, I was being watched by the paper's advertising director, Karen.

Nobody gets somewhere completely on her own. Those who say they have are simply choosing their ego over integrity. I am what they call "self-made," but that is just shorthand for someone who's been enabled by a small but resolute army. People who have cared for and believed in me. The people I call my "angels."

Karen was small, blond, an avid golfer, and what others in the industry referred to as a "ball buster." At the time, I was not aware that she was making it her pet project to groom me for a bigger role.

Karen promoted me into the Advertising & Sales Department by making me an advertising account executive soon after meeting me. On one of my first mornings on the job, she called from her door, "Michelle, come into my office."

When I walked in, she said, "Though I think your outfit is fashionable, you look like you're ready to go out, and it is not appropriate here."

I was wearing a white shirt draped over a burgundy camisole top, paired with Indian-print hip huggers dyed in rich, vibrant colors. I hadn't needed to develop a wardrobe working at the warehouse, so I didn't have anything office appropriate. I had borrowed this outfit from my fashionista girlfriend.

"Ours is a more conservative work environment, and I expect you to dress accordingly, in business attire," Karen said. "Go home and change."

I would later, while building my magazine career, perfect and love the style I was wearing that day—but that morning, I put it back in the closet, utterly humiliated. Still, I respected Karen, even when she handed out such punches to my ego, and I learned as fast as she was teaching me.

My job entailed selling advertising space, and I got a client group nobody wanted to touch: the restaurants. To my colleagues, they were at the bottom of the barrel, something beneath them. Coming from a range of ethnicities, many of my clients spoke very little English. I took the challenge. While experiencing food from all around the world, I fostered meaningful relationships with these restaurant owners, learning about their cultures, families, and dreams, and figuring out how I could assist in making their businesses more successful.

———

After a couple of years, Karen retired. In parting, she told me, "The newspaper business is too conservative for you. You should move into magazine publishing. I have a friend who is looking for an account executive, and I can make the call if you are interested."

That is how I started with *Diablo* magazine, where Barney and Steve—two men whom I to this day consider my angels—would teach me everything I came to know about magazine publishing, and where I got to feel the wind swell under my wings.

Barney was my boss and an extraordinary advertising director. Steven was the magazine's founder and publisher, and let's just say I wanted to be him. He was charismatic, handsome, stylish, brown, and preeminent. He had built a successful magazine by defying the naysayers and disrupting the status quo. And he was an active and committed divorced dad to his two boys.

After about five years with *Diablo*, I left the full-time role and started doing special projects for them, such as launching new publications. At the same time, I started my own regional gay-and-lesbian magazine with my savings, which was all of $400. (To put that time into perspective, the LGBT market was still somewhat of a unicorn, and *Out* magazine had yet to make its debut.)

I had one employee and was pretty much doing everything while being silently mentored, through their books, TV appearances, and any stories about them that hit the media, by two astounding women: Oprah Winfrey and Grace Mirabella, the editor of *Vogue* magazine.

When it came to my lift-off, Grace picked up where my parents, Karen, Barney, and Steve left off. She was doing a book signing at Saks Fifth Avenue, in San Francisco's Union Square, and I did something quite out of character for me: I stood in a line of some thirty women who separated me from her, waiting for them to extricate themselves from my path one by one.

Grace was sitting behind this table, her little glasses attached to one of those bead strings that women employ once they grow into bigger things to worry about than where they put their spectacles. To her right towered a thick Russian woman in a red Chanel dress. To her left was a stack of her books, *In and Out of Vogue*. She automatically reached for the next one the instant the woman before me swayed out of my way.

"What would you like me to write in your book?" Grace asked without even looking up.

I dropped to my knees and put my arms on the table. "You don't have to put anything in my book. Just the fact that I got to meet you is a dream come true."

Grace was one of those people who had reached her heights in an unconventional manner. A regular Jersey girl, she had ascended to change the face of fashion, and to make it accessible to everyday women. Like Oprah, she was a pioneer. She was what I was going to figure out how to become.

Grace looked up. Grounded. Grand. Gracious. Later, she told me that it was my big brown eyes, bottomless and relentless, that compelled her to engage. The eyes are the window to the soul, just like my mother always said.

"You must be in the business," Grace said.

"If I could ask for anything, my next dream would be to buy you a cup of coffee when I make it to New York."

The Russian was getting scarier, audibly clearing her throat with her folded arms hefty and restless in my peripheral vision as I stared right at Grace.

She gazed back at me and put her hand out. "Deal."

We shook on it, firmly and intently.

Grace gave me her card but then took it right back, saying, "You'll never get to me through the office. Call me on this number." She wrote down her home phone in my book and handed it back.

I floated out onto Union Square, full of disbelief and gratitude, and let a bench hold me while I sobbed, all the while clutching that precious volume, its first page holding a promise in Grace's handwriting: "Until we meet in New York."

———

A month went by and I still hadn't called Grace. I couldn't bring myself to dial the number and discover that it was wrong, or that she couldn't speak to me. I would not allow myself to spoil the illusion that Grace Mirabella herself cared for me, and was waiting for me in New York.

And then she called me. "Hey, kid. It's Grace Mirabella."

I couldn't believe my ears, or my mouth, as I confirmed that I would indeed meet her for tea at four o'clock at the Cliff House on the day she was due back in San Francisco.

One of the first things she asked when we sat down was, "So, why aren't you living and working in New York?"

My life, what I was going to become, was bigger than San Francisco, and I knew it. But I also knew that I had at least one problem. I was embarrassed to tell her, but I was honest: "I don't have an advertising or journalism degree."

We talked for hours. It must have been past 7:00 a.m. when she said she had to get some sleep before showing up at the TV studios of *Good Morning America*, the reason for her trip to the West Coast.

"I have worked with hundreds of people in New York, and you are just as good as any of them," she said. "You will do great there. You have the heart and drive of a New Yorker. Let me make a couple of calls."

She set up an interview for me in LA with Condé Nast. I was on the plane within days.

———

Fifteen minutes into my interview at Condé Nast, the HR person who was conducting it disappeared for "a minute"—which turned into twenty—before reappearing to say, "Grace is right about you. You need to be in New York."

She proceeded to tell me that somebody would contact me to make arrangements. They were already made by the time I turned my phone back on upon touchdown in San Francisco. My flight to New York was booked, and I had barely twenty-four hours before takeoff—during which time I needed to figure out what I was going to wear into the offices of only the most prestigious fashion magazine in the world.

My mom went shopping with me to find an outfit. "I have an interview with Condé Nast," I told the salesperson at the department store, still startled by the whirl of events that seemed at once unbelievable, eternally anticipated, and utterly overdue.

Once on that United flight, I stayed in my seat for over thirteen hours, six of them spent on the tarmac in Oakland. By the time I stepped into my Shoreham hotel room, it was 2:00 a.m.

Just five hours later, a car picked me up and deposited me safely outside 350 Madison Avenue. I stepped into the lobby of Condé Nast wearing white pants and a bright orange shirt, my hair up like I was born for the sixties, my favorite era in apparel. My interview was to be with Jill from HR, but, again, it lasted barely fifteen minutes before I was left alone—for "a moment," of course.

"Okay, come on." Jill's voice jolted me right out of the thick, sticky fatigue that had nearly gotten the better of me. "You're coming with me."

I followed Jill closely while we passed many of the Condé Nast brand's offices—each space unique, enclosing a distinct universe with its own aspirations and rules—before reaching a private elevator that took us eleven floors above everybody else.

We entered a vast office. I was placed on a couch in a quasi–living room. A man whose significance I did not comprehend was screaming at whomever was unfortunate enough to be fused to the other end of the line. I was keenly aware of my heart pounding inside my chest.

When he put that phone down, he came over to me and sat down. "Now, tell me," he said, "how did you get to me?"

"Jill brought me up." In my head, I added, *After I waited for her for half an hour downstairs.*

"That's not what I'm asking. *Vogue* is a fine-tuned machine, and I am the very last person you almost never meet."

A few words between us, and my nauseating nerves were gone. He was good. Relaxed. Engaging. Exuding confidence and eliciting a sense of kinship. Raised by a single mom in a one-bedroom apartment in Queens, he came from humble beginnings. So we talked on.

He was Ron Galotti, the publisher of *Vogue*, the pinnacle of all Condé Nast properties. But I would realize that only later, when I looked him up back at the hotel. That morning in his office, I was very tired but pumped up by the city of my dreams and, yes, cocky.

"Look. I will get here with or without you, so you might as well hire me. Or somebody else will." My parting words.

What followed was a relay of about a dozen interviews. I was the baton, for the next eight hours, handed over from advertising director to associate publisher and everybody in between. Denise Fierro was one of them. *Vogue's* advertising director, she became a friend whom I later consulted about starting *And Baby Magazine.*

Once I was finally ejected from the building, without an answer or a sense of next steps, I was exhilarated as much as dehydrated. Efficient and thorough—that was how they did things at *Vogue*. Nobody had even offered me a glass of water.

From the hotel, I called Grace.

"I am not surprised they kept you all day," she said. "But I am not sure that's the best place for you. May be too corporate."

Over the course of the following months my phone would ring from *Rolling Stone*, *Maxim*, *Details*, *Brides*, and more.

That endurance race set off a ricochet of trips to New York, where I was shaken out, peeked through, reviewed, labeled, and passed along the conveyor belt of the Condé Nast interview process. I pounded the pavement of Madison Avenue, intermittently interviewing at various other magazines that Grace launched at me.

The process included reference checks, which I discovered when one of my former clients called me for a brief catch-up on life, work, and family and said, "So, *Vogue* magazine called me about you. They asked me a bunch of questions."

"What did you say?" I asked.

"I said, 'You can drop Michelle anywhere in this world, and within two months she will be established. She will have friends, clients, a life—the lot of it.'"

Her genuinely glowing reference, unsolicited by me, made me proud of what I had done and replenished my confidence. I came to learn that nearly everyone I had ever worked with had been contacted, and all of them had given me highly complimentary reviews.

Despite the fact that eleven of Condé Nast's nineteen properties were hiring in sales, I only met with two of them; *Vogue* had decreed a freeze on me, preventing anybody else from making a move on me until they did. "The Mercedes of the magazine industry," indeed.

After six months of thorough scrutiny, *Vogue* passed on me.

During this time I had witnessed, my hands tied and lips muted, other ambitious go-getters staking their claim to juicy positions at *Mademoiselle*, *Allure*, and *Glamour*. Man, was I pissed off—my personality's disguise for being hurt and feeling broken, rejected. But then my father's voice burst into my head, as always: "You are knocked down but not knocked out, so get up and off that mat, champ! Keep fighting!"

After all, I did have two offers.

The only other Condé Nast property I had met with was *Condé Nast Sports*. The business manager liked me and took me to lunch, where he let me in on the freeze, announced that he couldn't make a move (which he seemed to regret as much as I did), and told me about *Paper Magazine*. Then he made a call to the publisher, Kim Hastreiter.

Kim called me at home, herself, because she was coming to the West Coast, and shortly thereafter I was on a plane to LA to meet her at Chateau Marmont.

I was taken aback by Kim. She was real, not the typical, precisely fashioned industry person. Her humble beginnings resonated with me. She had started *Paper* as a free handout, run out of her apartment, and grown it into a fashion oracle. No serious brand or industry publication could afford to ignore *Paper* now, and every up-and-coming designer, actor, or artist prayed to it because Kim could singlehandedly make you. If you got covered by *Paper*, you were on your way to stardom and your life would never be the same.

I committed my loyalty to her when, the authority that she was, Kim dismissed my lack of formal education. All that mattered to her were my ability and tenacity, which I would give her in spades over the next few years.

When it was time for me to hop back to San Francisco, Kim drove me to the airport herself.

"I will be sending you an offer," she said as she dropped me off. "I want you to come work for me."

Within a week, I knew she was true to her word: her offer included my move to New York and six months of accommodation in Manhattan, and it boasted a good salary with a fantastic commission bonus, not to mention access to everything and everybody that mattered within the fashion industry.

The second offer was from another privately held publishing company. I would collect a bigger salary there than I would with *Paper*, work right out of my loft south of Market Street in San Francisco, and travel to New York only once a quarter.

That was the offer that had the vote of my mother—of everybody in my big, assertive family, really, at least those who cared to make their advice known to me.

Then my dad asked me to lunch.

"Get whatever you want, bebe," he said when we sat down. He was a regular at the restaurant and treated the staff like family.

The food was great, authentic, home-style. With my internal argument in full flight, my fork moved on autopilot until my father's advice summoned my mind to attention.

"Get the hell out of here, champ." Present, considered, kind, he was looking into my eyes. "If you hang out with the snakes, you become a snake. San Francisco isn't going anywhere, you can always come home. But for now, leave the snake pit. Please, take the offer and go."

That was my dad—giving his baby the best advice I ever got.

Within a few weeks, I was a New Yorker.

———

It was Saturday, February 8, when I landed in New York with a drop-roots rather than a carry-on. The rest of my stuff was in transit. And it was absolutely freezing.

There is no way I could have prepared myself for the New York brand of cold. The type that ignored any clothing I amassed and bored all the way to my bones. It took me six months to get warm. Apparently, that's how long it took for my blood to thicken. And for me to learn to layer like an East Coaster.

That Sunday, I was sad in a café on Sixth Avenue. Overnight, it had hit me that I did not know any of the hundreds of people passing by me every few minutes, all preoccupied in a life that had no connection with mine. Planning and travel now barricaded the space between me and my family. I missed my parents' couch, and all the great times I was not going to share with my sisters. And even more so, I was grieving over the distance that was yet to grow between us now that my life had become altogether different. Even if for no other reason than that I was going home to my loft on Seventeenth and Sixth.

By the next morning, however, my excitement over entering what had been my dream helped me step into who I was born to be, stashing for safekeeping the remnants of the melancholy and uncertainty I had experienced the night before. That Monday, I was at my new office at Broadway and Spring Streets in SoHo. The headquarters of *Paper Magazine*. Decked out with style. Filled with authority. Busting with the need to prove something.

My title was Advertising Manager for American and European Beauty and Fragrance. I had an assistant and thirty clients that were already regular. My pool included six hundred top brands that I would proceed to activate and serve. At *Vogue*, a much more structured machine, I would never have had this broad a platform; I would have been working either beauty or fashion, my scope either American or European. That's why I felt so loyal to Kim: she bestowed upon me a whole realm, while *Vogue* would have given me only a position.

By Tuesday, as was my (new, utterly changed) place, I was sitting between Kim and Bette Midler (yes, that one) in the front row of the Bryant Park New York Fashion Week. Bette held her fan in front of her face the entire time, totally matter of fact. She uttered not a word the whole show—not even a "hi" or a "hey, move over." It was quite weird. She exuded the accomplishment and authority of an icon.

That's when I noticed Ron Galotti making a beeline toward me from the entrance.

"You are going to leave me, aren't you?" Kim said, spotting him. "You are going to leave me!"

Kim's anxiety hadn't transferred to me before I lifted off my seat into his elegant greeting, an embrace that began with both of my cheeks getting a kiss, classy and European, and concluded with his gaze straight on mine.

"What are you doing here?" he asked.

"I told you I was going to get here with or without you." I smiled and stared straight into his eyes.

My mind plunged me back into that daylong interview and replayed parts of the last exchange, which was with the associate publisher. "We have a way here," he told me. "A way we do things and promote people. I am not afraid that you cannot do the job. What I am afraid of is that within six months, you will be bored with your position and will be able to do your boss's job, and what do I do with you then?"

Though they were not a union shop, there was a particular way that things worked at *Vogue*. You worked your way up. At the time I was bitter about that, but now, as a business owner, I get it. I was a wild card that would have disrupted their status quo.

Back in the celebrity-filled hall, Ron was still standing in front of me. "You will be hearing from my people," he told me before walking away. He sounded like a mafia dude.

Vogue did indeed start calling me after that event—first at the office and then on my unlisted home number, which I still have no idea how they got. Again, very "mafia."

That's when they made me an offer. A big, fat, sumptuous offer.

One of the best days of my life followed shortly after: the day I turned it down. I was going to be loyal to Kim. And my time at *Paper* would have lasted much longer than the few years I ended up spending there had I not felt so out of step with the others—had I still partied. But I would always be the only one, to the expressed shock of my assistant, who started work before eleven o'clock in the morning. Namely, by 7:00 a.m.

———

I had a headache for the first three weeks of my New York tenure because of the noise, which ranged from a startling screech to a buzz but was omnipresent. Inescapable. When some people say they have a headache, like in the commercials, what they really mean is they get a headache, take a pill, and feel it subside. Given my sobriety, I try to stay away even from aspirin, so I genuinely had that headache for weeks, felt every pulling and nauseating cramp of it through my brain.

That's when my counterpart, aka Advertising Manager for American and European Beauty and Fashion (Men), gave me a valuable piece of advice.

"You have got to just get in your car and drive up Highway 80," he told me.

"Isn't that the one we have in California?"

"It goes all the way through," Hunter pointed out affectionately.

"Oh."

A couple of days and a few dozen miles later, I had myself an oasis: a special place on the Delaware River in Pennsylvania. I was startled by how secluded and nascent it was, only an hour and a half from NYC. It was authentic despite adjoining the capital of wannabe. Lusciously green and self-contained, Milford was to counterbalance my new, high-fashion world.

I became a regular there, following its pull on the weekends, especially when the stress became debilitating. I would go skinny-dipping in the river and make a day out of hanging out in the little town. And I always passed through my favorite—and Milford's only—diner.

"What do you do?" I asked a woman sitting at the next table one day. She was busy making and reading notes in between forkfuls of breakfast. I had noticed her several times now, and she seemed like a local.

"Well, I'm a real estate agent," she said.

Without even realizing what I was doing, I exposed myself as a potential client as we talked. We chatted for over an hour and continued our dialogue over a few more unplanned brunches in the months to come. I asked her to keep an eye out for a fixer-upper for me to purchase—a place with good bones that wasn't too expensive. I wasn't desperate for a property, but I was interested in buying something I could make whole. She promised to look out for opportunities.

———

During the workweek, Kim introduced me to the world of fashion and New York; who's who and what's what, what's hot and what's not. Kim was, and is still, after all these years, a barometer for the fashion industry.

Wherever Kim appeared, she was engulfed in an instant, as if her presence created a vacuum that sucked everybody into it. I had a backstage pass to everywhere, was welcomed at Betsey Johnson's house, had conversations on the street with Todd Oldham, chatted with Donna Karan, and met a number of celebrities and celebrity bands. I no longer heard that I must be from "someplace else" because I talked or walked too fast. And I got to walk to work every day, through Union Square, wearing a formidable wardrobe without ever having to shop.

I didn't register the moment it happened, but all of a sudden I was no longer new to New York. The bodegas, the noise; my loft, the telepathic coordination taxies had with my schedule; the indifferent crowds moving at hectic speeds; all of it treated me as one of its own and felt intimately familiar. It seemed impossible that I ever felt otherwise.

For the first time in my life, my surroundings matched that which filled me inside. I had always been wired for this city, and now I was synched with its beat. I had never felt more at ease.

CHAPTER 2:
WHEN ONE BECAME TWO

FANTASY: an imagined or conjured up sequence fulfilling a psychological need; daydream.

"Hello! Anybody there?"

My friend and I were sitting at the bar, supposedly catching up, but I was the only one talking. She gave me a dull, *What do you want from me!?* look in return.

I was really tired. I had just returned from Santa Barbara the night before, where it had been a busy ten days of deadlines for a client's magazine. I really hadn't wanted to leave my loft, but my friends had been adamant about me showing up at our regular, Ruby Fruits in Greenwich Village, to hang. I hadn't seen them for some time; work had been all-consuming lately. So what the heck, I had decided to go.

"Come on, man," I complained. "I've asked you all sorts of questions and I get nothing; you keep staring at that door like it's gonna win you a jackpot."

A lesbian bar, Ruby Fruits was shaped long and skinny, sort of like a railroad apartment. The walls were covered with pictures of joyous women—most celebrities, some lesbians, and all proud and free. Many of us locals hung out there; it was an iconic mainstay of the Village and a happy empowering place for any woman.

In particular, a two-woman cover band that played at the bar on Thursday nights was something to look forward to each week; they were beautiful and passionate and always put on a show. It was a good time for all—a lot of laughs, chatter, and, of course, flirting.

"Hey, dude, I'm here, okay?" my companion finally said. "No fuss. Just waiting for a friend who's on the way; she's a tight-ass—oops, I meant 'budget conscious.' Forty-five minutes ago she told me she was looking for a parking spot, which means she has been driving around since then. But she's great."

Regardless of what I said, or asked, our catch-up was suspended for a few more minutes, until I finally heard, "Thank god! There she is."

I looked at the entrance door. A woman walked in and was making her way through the crowd, moving with ease and a sort of simplicity.

My friend made the introduction: "M, this is X; X, this is M."

We exchanged glances but didn't say a word to each other.

I felt an instant, overwhelming familiarity, as if I had known X for years. She was beautiful, with dark hair and hazel eyes. She, however, didn't give me the time of day. While most women seemed uncomfortable—nervous, even—in my presence (which was always a turnoff), X had a quiet, standoffish confidence about her. I had had many NGFs (non-girlfriends), and none had reacted to me or affected me in this way. I admit I was a bit stumped, but more than that, I was enamored with and allured by X.

Life plowed along. I was bicoastal by this point, and I flew back to California within days.

I had concluded my stint at *Paper Magazine*. While it had been an amazing experience, my clients and colleagues expected to do business in the many luxurious lounges and bars of NYC, and their late nights were generously lubricated with alcohol and more. My issue wasn't temptation; I had made my choice. It was the omnipresence of others past intoxication points that was getting to me. If you have ever been the designated driver, you know that the fun had by your chatty, drunk friends is much less tantalizing to the sober you.

I had also discovered that my dream job, in my dream city, hadn't been as satisfying as I had imagined it would be. It wasn't the business nor the impact of fashion that disappointed me. The hard-working designers inspired me. To me, they were the original revolutionaries. By abolishing corsets, removing those butt enhancers from dresses, or introducing practical dress cuts, they had won the silent revolution for women's value before its intellectual underpinnings gained traction. The styles of the fifties and of Motown inconspicuously wove African American culture into the mainstream and seeded the racial revolution. To me fashion, like art, has always been the mirror of society; without saying a word, it gives voice even to the most clandestine ideas.

I also found the business of high fashion to be an unsung hero of the American dream. Many of the industry icons, I learned, had risen from nothing through sheer tenacity. For example, Giorgio Armani had started off commuting by bike to his job sewing buttons.

Furthermore, I deeply admired Kim for her ability to spot and legitimize potential in people and ideas. She truly kept the wheel of US fashion churning.

I marveled, too, at how the greats could elevate and preserve history just as they moved us forward. A classic cannot be premeditated. It succumbs to obsolescence or endures at the whim of (often accidental) repurposing, as when a designer or a connoisseur renews the meaning of an older cut or pattern. Once established, classics hold the power to instantaneously connect us to an epoch and its ethos. Classics steady us against Time's capricious breath.

Despite what I loved about fashion, however, I also grew to recognize and despise the ugly underbelly of the industry. The falseness that gravitated into its powerful vortex. Posturing accolades. Hollow models. The fanatical copycatting of "the look." Miserable women forgoing paying rent in order to buy a $500 pair of shoes.

Had I still partied, I might have glossed over the phony loyalties and paper-thin affections of this insular world. After all, the industry institutionalized all forms of vices because they made bearable the insecurities, the hunger, and the loneliness. Today, both the fashion and entertainment industries are actually budging in their ways to accommodate the many celebrities that are proudly clean and sober. But twenty years ago, we were few and far between.

So, just as my career was on the rise, I quit, though nobody besides my mother and closest friends understood my decision. To this day, I fondly and gratefully remember those years of beauty, access, learning, achievement, and good times. But it was time for me to chart my own path.

———

I quickly picked up a handful of contracts: branding and packaging for private clients on the East Coast, and publishing consulting on the West Coast.

New York was home, anchored in my beautiful penthouse on the water with a view of the city.

I was also living ten days per month in Santa Barbara, California, where I had a quaint two-bedroom bungalow half a block from the beach. My California client wasn't bad either. I was getting paid well to do interesting work: launching a new magazine for an untapped, niche market. This would soon become my specialty.

The only craving of my heart that was unmet at the time was for a dog. There has always been a place for a dog in my life. There are as many views about pets as there are people in the world, but for me, my dogs have always been an extension of the Universe's caring hand. I believe they have souls and, spared all the vanity of the human mind, are pure conduits to guide and nurture us along our journeys in "Earth School."

My parents had always had dogs, all off-leash trained and big personalities, but I got the first four-legged companion of my own when I was ten. My sister had acquired an English springer spaniel, and by the time her first litter was due, I was dying for a puppy. AKC-certified and $75 a pop, the puppies were too expensive for my parents, so I tried to earn one—and on Easter day, my brother-in-law brought me a priceless bundle of a gift: Snow, one of those coveted puppies.

Snow became my best friend and saw me through my early twenties, when I experienced the loss of having the vet put her down. What followed was a series of black labs, some that I found, others that found me. The last was Madison—Madison Avenue Darné. She was still a puppy when I moved to New York with *Paper Magazine*. My intention was to send for her as soon as I settled into my own place, of course finding accommodation that allowed dogs. But that was not to be.

One day, my assistant told me that my mother was on the line. I was in a meeting with Kim, but she said, "Just take it, it's okay."

"This fuckin' dog!"

My mother's unabashed anger erupted through the speaker, and Kim strained to contain a smile. Madison had managed to flood my mother's yard—my mother's unbelievably gorgeous, envy-inducing gardens—by turning on the spigot.

Having jeopardized that relationship, Madison took to

running off. One day, a gentleman brought her back and teared up during the handover. Soon after, I got a call from my sister. "Sis, I know you want to send for Madison. But I gotta tell you, Mr. Davis is in love with that dog. His wife is really ill, and you should have seen his eyes when he brought her back. It was like it was breaking his heart."

Perhaps Madison was always meant to be Mr. Davis's dog, I thought; I decided I had to let her go. And now, with all the travel between two places where I had no family, it just wasn't the right time to get a puppy.

Otherwise, though, life was good. I was making good money and saving much of it. Working hard, playing hard, and enjoying a few handpicked rituals.

In California, there was surfing. I am an early riser and would often get up at the crack of dawn, go straight to my coffee machine, and then off to enjoy the surf. By the time my meetings started around 10:00 a.m., I would have had my ocean time, a couple of cups of java, and time to do a strategic scan of both global and industry news. Not much short of paradise.

In New York, I played sports and spent time with friends. On Tuesday nights I played softball, and Friday nights were carved out for soccer at the RockStar stadium. Three times a week, my alarm was set for 5:00 a.m. so that I could be at Brooklyn's Gleason's Boxing Gym by 6:00 a.m. The place gave me a particular sense of family. You should have seen us spar, my trainer and I, to the sound of chuckles and teasing from other regulars. I had a presence, but he was six feet tall and three hundred pounds. I called him Tiny. He called me Big.

Sundays have always been special. I read *The New York Times* Sunday edition religiously, and during those years always followed that up with a brunch with close friends. I cooked, gladly and with the luscious ingredients of the next-door farmers' market, for whomever could come, or whomever was sleeping off the previous night's outing on my couches. It was our time, and my time, to slow down, silence the stress, and soak in New York, at once my companion, my catalyst, and my sanctuary—like no other place in the world.

And whenever I was in New York, Thursdays featured Ruby Fruits.

———

Over the course of the next six months, X and I saw each other occasionally, always among a group of friends. Through several casual conversations, we got to know a bit about each other.

X was different than anyone I had ever dated. She appeared to have a normal life, if there is such a thing. She was a graphic designer, living with two housemates and working eight to five for an ad agency in Jersey. I was drawn to the simplicity of her life, and of her dreams. While associated with the creative industry, she was a step removed from it. Her weekends were always her own and included puttering around at home or spending time with her friends. Her life appeared steady and non-stressful.

I, on the other hand, was an over-the-top Type A personality in the thick of building a business, living between two coasts, and working fourteen to sixteen hours per day, except for Sundays. I was committed to proving that I could succeed and build the company of my dreams.

Neither circumstance was better or worse than the other, just different. I believe that difference is what brought us together.

I moved quickly to clean out my life. I wanted to be available to date her with no distractions, so I let go of the few people I was seeing at the time.

For our first official date, we went to a hip downtown restaurant in SoHo. It was fun; we chatted about our personal lives and what we wanted for the future. I liked her a lot, and I loved the fact that with her, for the first time I was discussing something other than work. I felt like we really connected on a human level. I left that dinner with a new spring in my step, and a pulling desire to see her again.

We had one big thing in common: we both wanted a family.

"Do you hope to have kids some day?" I asked during one of our early conversations.

"Yeah, that has always been a dream of mine. My biggest dream, in fact."

Whenever I asked whether she had other dreams, such as to travel the world or achieve a particular height in her career, she shrugged it off.

"No," she said. "Work's not that important to me. I just want to have a family. A stable life and children."

The women I had dated before were in the industry; they were successful or aspiring actresses or models, every one as self-absorbed as the last. Children were the furthest thought from their minds. X, on the other hand, held a promise of a lifelong bond and family.

Whenever we planned to see each other, I would feel sick in my stomach—nauseated, actually. I swear, many a time I thought I would throw up right on her shoes.

We were spending a lot of time together, and my idiosyncrasies were becoming more and more apparent. For example, I have always been a clean freak: I love for my environment to be beautiful, I love white, and I love having everything in its rightful place—flowers positioned perfectly in a vase and books arranged just right, even if they are stacked on the floor.

One day, X didn't wipe the sink after washing the dishes, and I freaked out about the water spots. It was undeniable: I was a weirdo! But X didn't seem to mind; she seemed okay, even gracious, about all that.

As a lesbian, I dare say I was more comfortable in my skin than X was. My inexplicably progressive mother "outed" me when I was twelve, and the stereotypes about both the fashion and the entertainment industry went on to hold pretty true for me: a lot of us were gay, and alternative lifestyles were a norm. And while law and policy had not kept pace with society, being lesbian in NYC was a nonissue; in fact, in Brooklyn, where I lived, it was kind of hip.

X, on the other hand, hadn't come out to her parents until she was about thirty-two, and I was the first woman she ever introduced to them.

———

X lived an hour and a half away from me, which easily became a two-and-a-half-hour trip in traffic. When the company where she worked was sold, they made her an offer to stay, but she decided to take a severance package and leave. She used her accumulated vacation time at the end of her time there, and she chose to spend it with me in New York.

My office was very busy with client work. The art department in particular was bottlenecking because my business partner, who headed up the creative team, was on vacation, and we were short on graphics expertise. X offered to come in for a few days to help out.

My staff loved her and her work.

"Please, can we keep her?" they kept asking, basking in her talent. While she didn't go, she had been accepted to the Philadelphia Academy of Art, one of the most prestigious art schools in the country and a testament to her ability.

It was like a mantra, resonating quietly but obstinately through the office: *Keep her! Keep her! Keep her!*

So we "kept her," and she proved to be one of the best employees I have ever had: she was well versed in technology as well as in the old-school way of designing, conscientious, and never missed a deadline.

———

As X and I got closer, I felt it was time to have the two most prominent women in my life spend some time together. I chose the ocean and vast skies of Southern California for the backdrop, and invited X to join me on one of my routine trips to Santa Barbara, where my mother would meet us for a couple of days. My mom absolutely adored Santa Barbara and had frequently come to spend time with me there, so I knew she'd be comfortable; plus, the two-hour flight from the Bay Area was significantly easier travel than coming to the East Coast.

Our first morning there, I headed off to work and left X and my mom to spend the day together. They walked around for hours, doing some light shopping up and down State Street, had lunch, and met me back at my place for dinner.

"Your mom talked to me quite a bit," X told me later that night, once we were alone again.

I could imagine that. X wasn't much of a talker, while my mom thrives on engagement. She would have been telling stories, going for a laugh here and there, asking questions, and trying everything to draw X in.

"She told me some of her story," X said. "She really did have a tough life. And tough for me to hear." She sounded exhausted, in fact.

"Yes, she did," I said. "She is amazing, right?"

"She also told me how you got sober."

"Oh, okay," I said, processing that. I guessed that my mother wanted X to be cognizant of what it means to be with an addict, so that she could be both respectful and prepared. "Is there anything you'd like me to explain, fill in?"

"No, no. It all happened before me, I don't really need to know."

That was nearly the extent of our interaction about that aspect of my life.

———

Back in New York, I got a call from my Milford real estate agent one morning.

"Hi!" she said. "I think I have something you will love."

It had been about a year since I had discovered Milford. Curiously, X was the only one I had ever mentioned Milford to who knew—and loved—it. Everybody else had never heard of the place. Yet another reason why I felt she was the perfect one for me.

"The house sits on a whole acre and a half of land, secluded, like you insisted, and needs some of that love you had to offer," the agent said. "Good bones."

Her energy reignited the pull that Pennsylvania had over me.

"This is your ideal house. And the best part is, it isn't on the market yet—not officially. You have to, you absolutely must, come see it right away."

My weekend plans got made that second. X went with me to view the property. We headed out of NYC early on Saturday. It was a stunning morning, and, with us chatting all the way up Highway 80, the drive went by very fast. We had breakfast at the diner and then headed up to view the house.

The property was six miles out of town on Highway 6. It was so private that we missed the driveway the first time around. Sitting on a meadow at the end of a private, tree-lined road, withdrawn and engulfed in an acre of dense forest, the house looked like a small barn. As soon as I saw it, I knew it was our house. Without having set foot inside, I saw it finished, dignified, and beautiful.

In reality, the house was pretty beat up. It had sat empty for three years and was definitely in need of some serious TLC. The Veterans Association owned it, but raccoons appeared to be the only ones frequenting the place.

"Are you sure you want this place?" I remember X asking me upstairs, in the master bedroom.

I was. I had found the fixer-upper I had been looking for.

As we drove back to NYC, we started the discussion about buying it together. I had the cash for the down payment and was willing to take on the responsibility of the monthly mortgage payment, and she had the credit to get the loan approved.

I thought that having a house in the country would be good for us both, but especially for X. She had told me numerous times that living in New York had never been on the radar for her. Having come from a small town, she wasn't much of a city girl and had no desire to become one.

We made an agreement that if the relationship went sour we would sell the house and split the proceeds. We closed on the property within a month, in the week of X's birthday, and were both a bit shocked that it all happened so quickly and smoothly. We were happy, to say the least.

I decided to throw X a surprise birthday party. I figured that in addition to giving her joy, this would be a good opportunity to integrate our friends and for me to meet her family. I enlisted a couple of her friends to help me make contact with the important people in her life. This seemed to me like a good time to also let her parents know that we had bought a house in the country, as this would show them how serious we were about each other and how much I cared about X. I was nervous and excited about meeting these people who I hoped would eventually be my in-laws.

I had said to the girls helping me organize the party that they should invite whomever they saw fit, and they included X's ex-boyfriend. Curiously, X spent the party in the kitchen, holding hands with him. I didn't mind, however, let alone find it threatening; from what she had said and from what I was seeing, he seemed to be one of those types you leave more often than you marry.

At the end of the party, X's father came up to me. He was average height with big blue eyes, jovial, and kind.

"Michelle, it's really great that you bought the house in Pennsylvania. And it sounds like you got a great deal." He sounded energized by the party. "X is going to absolutely love it. At heart she's not a city girl, you know."

I don't think I ever knew for sure how X came to feel about the house. She ended up spending a lot less time there than I had anticipated. There was one time, however, when I got to see her really happy and present, and that happened to be about the house.

We were planning to spend the weekend in Milford, and X did not know that I had had the painting finished, or that I had asked our contractor to keep the lights on for our arrival that weekend. As we pulled up, she started crying.

"Oh my god," she exclaimed. "It is so-o-o beautiful!"

I made sure that she had an art area in the house, her own space. Italian food was our shared love, but the rest of our interests we pursued separately. We did always have dinner together. I would cook and we would banter about our day. Although our "banter" sounded like a work meeting more often than I would care to admit and I sometimes went back to the office after dinner, we always made an effort to take our last meal of the day together.

After X's birthday party, we started going to New Jersey every week to have dinner with her parents, and they always seemed happy to see us. Several months later, once the house was finished, they even came to spend the weekend with us.

It was evening; I was making adobo, one of my signature Filipino dishes. It involves cooking dark chicken meat for a long time in a broth of apple cider vinegar, soy sauce, and a bouquet of spices. It is a near-guaranteed hit that is actually not that difficult to make.

X and her dad left for the hardware store, as we were out of salt for the icy driveway, so it was just me and X's mother in the kitchen.

"I really didn't want to be alone in the house with you," she blurted out.

"Pardon me?" I asked, half thinking I hadn't heard her right.

"Well, you know, you and I don't have anything in common. The things you talk about, Africa, other countries, global issues . . . I am not interested in that."

"Okay," I said. I accepted her point of view and chose to focus on what we could both share. At that point, that was the craft of dinner, so I shifted gears to move us on.

"What you are looking for is for the chicken to start falling off the bone," I explained through the awkwardness, dismissing what I felt, hoping it was just a whiff of emotion.

I adored X's parents because I loved her and they were her family. I chose not to focus on our differences and grew to have quite a warm relationship with them.

———

For our first anniversary, which was in January, X and I gave ourselves the gift of Jackson the Labrador (a girl, the name notwithstanding). Picking our breeder was the only decision we got to make; after an unexpectedly scrutinizing interview process, she picked Jackson out for us, astutely looking for the most resilient puppy in the litter.

We met Jack as she was coming off the plane. She was a little peanut, jet black, a mere eight weeks old. Our first baby, she went on to be a frequent flier with Delta Dash, and to befriend the cargo staff of many airports. But that day, we were just falling in love and starting our journey together.

While I had X and now a best bud, Jackson, I was missing my mother. I was no longer traveling to California as much as I used to, and our rendezvous in Santa Barbara had come to a halt. So I arranged for my mom to come visit us in New York.

Unfortunately, despite my best planning efforts, something came up the day my mother arrived, and I had to stay at work late. I encouraged her and X to go ahead to Pennsylvania early, without me. I would catch up with them as soon as I could.

Later that night, I got a call from Mom.

"I need to go home now." She sounded determined.

"But, Mom . . . you just got here."

"I got *here*, and now I want to leave, please make the arrangements right away."

"Mom, talk to me, please."

"This house is ice cold."

During the winter months, we only kept the heat high enough to keep the pipes from freezing when we weren't there.

"So while waiting for the heater to ramp up, I turned the oven on to try to warm myself, but X came in and turned the darn thing off. I could not believe it!"

I knew why my mother was reacting this strongly. Having endured a childhood of poverty, often harboring the cold deep in her bones, my mother had vowed to herself to never compromise her physical needs like that again.

"Now X is hardly talking to me." I could hear my mother's voice quivering from hurt as much as from the cold.

I got X on the phone.

"Hey," she said. "Where are you?"

"I will explain everything when I get there, but for now please just run my mom a hot bath. I will be there shortly."

When I got in, my mom shared her trepidations about X. What had made her insensitivity worse for my mother was that X knew where she was coming from; earlier in the day, while driving from New York, my mother had ended up sharing that part of her life story with X.

"She seemed uncomfortable while I was telling her how it

used to be for me. I felt like I was talking to myself," my mother said, both upset and angry. "She has no compassion, this girl-friend of yours."

"Mom . . ."

"No! You need to know this. She is selfish! She is not what she says she is."

But I saw X differently, so I didn't listen; I didn't want to. Not counting the defiance of my youth, this was the first time I refused to hear my mother, and it pained me.

"I am sorry, Mom, but you're wrong," I told her. "This is the person I want to be with."

CHAPTER 3:
THE MAGAZINE

TRAILBLAZER: a pioneer in any field of endeavor.

"If anybody can do this, it's you," my mom said.

"But I'm scared, Mom. There is a lot of attention, chatter, scrutiny around me doing this, you know. People are saying some very nasty things—portraying me as the devil himself."

"Well, you know how it is: there are those who make things happen, and then there are armchair quarterbacks. Someone has to take a stand. If people aren't talking about you, hating on you, that means you are lazy. That means you are not making change. I raised you with tough skin, so it might as well be you."

"This first issue will determine whether the magazine is a go or no go."

"Finalize it and give it over to god, let it go. Trust that the Universe knows what to do with it."

I arrived in Milford determined to approve the final galley of the inaugural issue of my new project, *And Baby Magazine*.

———

It was 1999. I had been in the advertising and publishing business for twenty-odd years by this point, always working for mainstream magazines, from fashion to lifestyle. Now that X and I were talking about starting a family, I was dismayed to find that there were no national parenting magazines for the LGBT community. Only fragmented information was available, in part through one local publication that appeared to be in need of funding and advertising clients. There wasn't anything prominent—nothing with a strong national brand like *Parents* or *Baby Talk*. There was nothing that credibly spoke to our needs as a couple looking to start a nontraditional family.

And yet we had so many questions. Should we adopt? Use a donor we knew? Could I be on the birth certificate as the other parent? I knew in my gut that there were others just like us, puzzled and held back by endless lists of unanswered questions. And many others, less privileged than us, who were living under social taboos that would prevent them from even inquiring. So I started gathering information, doing my own market analysis.

In the business of high-stakes publishing there is an unspoken tenet nobody dares to deviate from: never publish a magazine for an untapped market, or any market that is not quantified by statistical data. What you do is replicate, with a twist, what is already published. For example, starting another sailing magazine or a slightly different yarn magazine would be considered a sound business decision, even if the strategy was simply to do it better than the other guys. But dare not venture into an unproven market.

I've never been good at following rules.

In its fourth year of operation, my consulting firm was solid enough to take on a special, self-funded project. In addition to that, most of its revenue was coming from publishing consulting, so I already had most of the skill set I needed. For years, we had been doing everything along the entire spectrum of magazine publishing. As part of my team, X was handling the creative for our clients' magazines when *And Baby* got added to the mix. At that stage, the only difference was that our work on our magazine wasn't behind the scenes. I owned the magazine, but for the team, it was just another project.

My first move was to engage my staff in research into the LGBT parenting market. It took about a year for me to see that it could be done. My team, including X, thought it was a good idea. Demand would be there, they advocated, and so would the advertising dollars. I had a range of discussions with some old ad agency clients, and they all affirmed that such a magazine needed to be done. Denise Fierro from *Vogue* was one of those sounding boards. All of them told me their advertising clients would definitely appreciate the opportunity once the data surfaced to quantify it. And they—as a testament to my recklessness as much as my ability, no doubt—contended that if anybody could pull it off, it was me.

So I became the publisher of *And Baby Magazine: Redefining Modern Parenting.* Just imagine the nightmare in trademarking anything starting with "and," but my amazing, relentless trademark attorney managed to get it done. My career was about to merge into the fast lane.

Initially, I was funding the project on my own. However, I knew that to do it justice, the magazine needed more than I could ever underwrite. I had to raise money. With that painful realization, I embarked on the up-and-down road I would traverse for the entire life of the magazine.

Our first investor was a completely unexpected result of a conversation where I came clean to a client who had repeatedly tried to hire me. I explained to him that I truly appreciated the offer but had this endeavor I was really passionate about—and he wrote me a check for fifty grand. This funded a few issues. Then he had me show up to a lunch he had set up.

"Just don't talk about *And Baby* unless they ask," were my arrival instructions.

They asked.

As we were leaving the restaurant, one of the guys put his arm around my shoulder. "What if I invested in Ms. Darné rather than the market?" he asked. "Hey, the market is tanking, isn't it?"

I grinned. "That would be fantastic!"

"How about $500,000?"

When my first investor and I got into the car, he was wearing a look of impressed disbelief. "Did you just close $500,000?" he exclaimed.

"Uh, I'm not sure . . ." I had never met the guy, so for all I knew he could have been joking around.

But the next day, he called me to say he was sending a check for $300,000, more than half of his commitment of $500,000. The check arrived, sent regular mail, in my mailbox three days later. No paperwork. Crazy times.

The entire office, X included, was thrilled. I was astonished, grateful, and all of a sudden in need of a good corporate attorney. That's when I engaged Chris, who became, hands down, one of my angels. He eventually helped me close a total of $1,750,000 in investment for *And Baby*, payable in installments of $250,000.

———

It was time to repurpose my consulting business. *And Baby* felt like a legacy project I was meant to do. Furthermore, it offered an indirect solution to an ongoing problem I was battling in my firm: to grow the business beyond myself. Every client stubbornly insisted on working directly with me, so I had a hard time handing accounts to others—which meant I was struggling to scale up. Phone calls and demands came at all hours and on weekends. While I cared for my clients and their businesses very much, and of course was grateful for the work, I often felt wholly owned by them and could not see an exit.

When I started running the two businesses simultaneously, it posed a huge problem for some of my clients. I had become the in-house-but-out-of-house branding guru for some, and they relied on me tremendously. They were on annual retainer agreements, renewable in December for the following year, so it took me over a year to phase them out—and it was actually quite hard, on me and on them. In a couple of cases, it felt like a breakup, and one client wouldn't speak to me for months afterward. I knew it was my fault: I had spoiled them and failed to set sound boundaries from the beginning.

While X told me she wasn't a creative director, I believed she could be, and I gave her the position with *And Baby*. Now we were deeply in it, together—our lives progressively intertwined.

Our relationship didn't feel like a dream come true, but I had adjusted my dream because it wasn't serving my future—a future in which I wanted companionship and children. X, and life with her, continued to offer promise of that future. She wasn't vain, career-obsessed, or disconnected from reality, like most of the women I had dated. She was real. I wanted to make her happy, to give her more experiences and things she had dreamed of. So what if in order to laugh, to regain a perspective over struggles, or to feel accepted, I would need to turn to my friends? I accepted that X and I would never do a number of things together, especially the public ones. All I needed to do, I decided, was to keep learning how to be happy with her for who she was, and with our life as a couple.

So I decided it was time to take the next step: I would ask her to marry me.

I proposed in Pennsylvania. I was so friggin' nervous! I hadn't slept all night leading up to it. I had already scouted the precise place by the river where I wanted to do it, but once we were driving together, though I drove to and fro (trying to make that seem nonchalant), I could not find it again!

I had to quickly scrap my preferred locale and conjure up a Plan B. I pulled over by the water, and we got out of the car.

"Like this river, our life moves, ebbs, and flows." I pointed to the water. "But the one thing we will continue to do together is move forward."

Lame, perhaps, but she sighed and nodded.

There were a few more jumbled words, she seemed graciously understanding, and lo and behold, we were engaged.

Gay marriage was still illegal. However, X and I felt it necessary to have our commitment ceremony among friends and family. Whenever we could make that happen, that is, as the magazine was all-consuming, and planning a wedding seemed nearly untenable.

Shortly after X and I got engaged, an irremediable crack in my relationship with my future in-laws formed.

At some point they had moved from New Jersey to Florida, as many East Coasters do when they retire. They came back up to visit, and X took them to the Pennsylvania house early in the week. To allow them plenty of time for catch-up, I didn't join them until late that Friday night, arriving after everybody was fast asleep.

The following morning I was out on the deck, reading the *The New York Times* with a cup of coffee, when X's mother came out. The others hadn't yet gotten up.

After a few silent moments in the early, misty, fresh morning, she spoke.

"There is a place in Florida, a great place we found for you. You and X could go there. Together."

"What do you mean?" I asked, my mind still contently absorbing the paper. I had not a clue what she was alluding to so carefully.

"Well . . ." She measured out her words. "A place where the two of you could go so that you are not like this with each other." Having overcome her initial awkwardness, she sounded energized by her discovery.

Struck with disbelief, I realized that hers was a pride over a solution she had found to cure our homosexuality.

As this sank in, I was flooded with disbelief. That feeling quickly morphed into repulsion.

Then rage.

"You *do* know that I have been out my whole life, don't you?" I demanded. The pain of betrayal was now displacing all other emotion. "I have no desire to be different!"

She stayed silent. Not knowing what else, if anything, could be said in that despicable situation, I excused myself from her presence and went inside.

The hours that followed left me feeling betrayed by my future in-laws. Two relationships I had held as true had been voided with just a few terrible, inconceivable, irretrievable words.

When X woke up and went to take a bath, I joined her in the bathroom and told her what had happened. She started crying, heartbroken.

This happened to be a time when I was receiving a lot of hate mail at *And Baby*, including numerous death threats from the conservative right, so I particularly counted on my inner circle for a sense of safety. On top of that, I felt used, taken advantage of under false pretenses. I was worthy when I was taking care of their daughter; when I was buying their airline tickets; when they were driving off in the Jeep I offered them to keep. My money was good enough, but I wasn't.

They tried to apologize, but only to and through X.

"We didn't really mean it that way," X would relate back on their behalf. However, I never felt they clarified what they *did* mean. If they did, I never grasped it. So if anything, those apologies only confirmed what I had heard on that deck.

I couldn't bring myself to stay, as planned, until Tuesday. I left on Sunday morning. Later, I told X that I no longer wanted to have anything to do with her parents. Going forward, they would only visit when I wasn't around. X was in a difficult position; though she was probably repeatedly hurt by their beliefs, she stayed close with them.

———

The tension I was experiencing at home made my professional successes at that time all the sweeter. *And Baby* was taking off like wild fire. It was the first national magazine focused on alternative parenting, and the target community across the US quickly embraced its content. *And Baby* was voted among the top ten new magazine launches of 2001, and it quickly rose to the top of all niche publications.

I sought to create a product that served the community. However, it was not just a product for them; *And Baby* was giving a wholesome and prominent voice to people historically silenced by prejudice and misunderstanding. It was legitimizing the experience of, the questions surrounding, and even the debate about alternative parenting.

In addition to normalizing, and formalizing, the hushed dialogue of society, *And Baby* could pose questions nobody else would dare explore. For example, we ran a feature story on male breastfeeding. Met with a gasp from the conservatives, its readership spanned a broad spectrum of people. Writing like this garnered us countless editorial accolades, including the prestigious Library Journal Association award. And I was proud of this, because of how I saw our mission.

And Baby was a dream for me as a publisher because it was groundbreaking across the board, from the audiences we served to the way we sold advertising.

"Uh-oh . . . sounds like you can see it," X used to say when another wild idea, having formed as a jumbled sketch, would appear in my imagination clear as a rendering. "That means you'll do it."

Fox News hailed me as the gay Martha Stewart (a label that fueled incessant teasing by my friends) because of the media empire I was building. *And Baby* was a living platform for advocacy that was as ardent as it was disarming.

The dominant argument at the time—dished out generously by the conservatives—involved contrasting gay and straight parenting. Despite numerous attempts to get me to chip in, especially on camera, I had no interest in that. A prime example was my appearance on *The Ananda Lewis Show*. She invited me along with a representative from Focus on the Family, a Christian-right group that had been running a scathing campaign against *And Baby* for months. That day, I found myself in the juicer of trash television (I despise trash programming); I was being pitted against the other guest, but I refused to get sucked in.

After the show, I was flooded with questions from our readers. "How did you manage not to blow up? I would have lost it!"

The truth was, that's what they wanted—to frame me as a crazy, vengeful, brown lesbian. And I couldn't give them that. I didn't feel that I had to shout our truth from the rooftops. Regardless of the volume of my voice, it would win ground if I focused on the similarities, not on the differences; if I stood in my power, as my mother would say.

I believe that was why we were also widely read by heterosexual parents. Whether we were straight, gay, prepared, accidentally knocked up, white, brown, green, or otherwise, as parents we all wanted to grow good kids. It might just look slightly different for all of us.

And Baby was smart and unapologetic. It was dancing its mission, embodying it as it provoked debate without alienating.

Servicing the mission of my magazine ignited a whole new layer of responsibilities for me. Most disenfranchised communities seek out their heroes. The alternative parents that united behind *And Baby* also sought to know and hail the person behind it. I was getting, through my publicist, numerous invitations to give interviews on the air and in the press, and they were increasingly focusing on me as an individual—on my backstory, values, and vision for the company. The office was also receiving a growing number of letters from our readership. Apart from a steady stream of bile from the conservatives, those letters told stories of happy families that *And Baby* helped make possible and expressed gratitude to me personally. I will always be thankful to those early adopters and their support.

I could not deny that the *And Baby* brand became stronger, reached farther, and commanded greater influence whenever we strengthened the Michelle Darné brand. From athletes to politicians and TV anchors, many people whose enterprises build in part on their personal vision or credibility experience this phenomenon. Along with *And Baby*'s recognitions of 2001, in the same year I was named one of the Top 100 Out People by *Out Magazine*. Shortly after, a journalist from *LA Weekly* followed me around for a whole day with the aim of exposing me as a person. She came away shocked that I effortlessly made us lunch from scratch, and reported, among other things, that I didn't apologize for who I was. (I found that curious, because I would never have thought to.) So, without ever intending to become a public figure, I emerged as the face of alternative parenting.

Pragmatically and without false humility, I accepted my

personal role in making *And Baby* a success. In hindsight, this placed a wedge between me and X.

I started doing quite a few media appearances. I was doing all the interviews, talking about X, our life, and our ambition for the magazine. Many interviewers would ask me smart-ass questions like, "Why should we believe you have a partner? We never see her!"

When we first started *And Baby*, I thought X would join me in some of the publicity appearances; I hoped she would stand next to me as we accepted the recognition of our community. But I came to view X as the antithesis of pretentiousness. She never showed any interest in the glitzy side of public life. Also, the reality was that we were on different schedules and she could not leave the office the way I could; her work was in the office just as much as mine was often outside its walls.

In the end, X agreed to walk the red carpet with me only once. It was for the Lace Awards in Hollywood, one of the most prestigious industry events of the year. She would wear a gown that had been custom-designed for her by an up-and-coming designer, and I would get to proudly walk with her toward the recognition that our work had garnered.

X had made me plenty aware that she didn't like my publicist: he was over the top. She was also outspoken about hating LA: it was pretentious. And she was exhausted from having flown into LA on a red-eye flight. So the whole setup began with a rocky start.

We were staying, as we always did, at Le Montrose, a quaint, private hotel in West Hollywood. When it was time to go, the town car was waiting for us outside, with my publicist already in the front seat. The moment we got in, he turned to us to rattle off how the evening would unfold. The driver would get out first, open the door for X, and escort her around the car. My publicist would next open my door and proceed to walk his usual three feet in front of us to seamlessly brief the press.

Even if they seem spontaneous and free-flowing, red-carpet events are tightly orchestrated; the luxurious calm of the arrivals is held together by unwavering precision. If your driver is given position four, he dare not deviate from that position upon arrival.

As my publicist rattled on, X grew increasingly livid, and my excitement of sharing the evening with her quickly gave way to nervousness and disappointment.

"Just smile," I said, trying to appease her. "It will be okay." I was trying to promise this to us both.

We stepped on the carpet. The cameras started flashing. I proudly took her hand and smiled at the press. She leaned over and hissed in my ear, "Don't you f***** *ever* make me do this again!"

For me, the flashing stopped and the exciting scene ahead shattered like glass. After a few pictures together, X was escorted inside while I was asked to stay for a few more shots on my own. I posed for the camera, a villain in the eyes of my wife but a hero in the eyes of the press—the citadel whose shoulders the community hoped to stand on.

———

Back then, my public persona was only just taking off. Frankly, I am not sure X ever saw my accidental publicity as a necessary means to an end rather than as my excuse to indulge myself. The same may be true of how she felt about our office.

Not only did I treat the publicity as a necessary by-product of my work, I didn't keep work at arm's length. For example, I treated my staff as family. I paid for car tires and bought Christmas gifts for my entire team. I was genuinely concerned about their well-being, regardless of their roles at work—in hindsight, perhaps too much so.

A few words about my "motley crew." (I have referred to my staff that way because nearly everybody was hired for—and worked to—their potential, not their qualifications.) It was us against the world, shaking up the way society viewed parenting.

When it became clear that *And Baby* was engulfing my branding and packaging business, my amazing assistant chose to take a different path (working for me, she had discovered a passion for research and landed a terrific offer from *Latina Magazine*) and was hiring her own replacement.

"Can you really smoke here?" This was the key question that my next assistant-to-be, Josh, asked his predecessor as she lit a cigarette during the interview.

"Yeah . . ." she said.

He grinned. "I absolutely *have* to have this job!"

Josh took over running my life with categorical powers. Flamboyant, fabulous, and brazen, he was my fierce gatekeeper. He also had a habit of launching himself at men he found irresistible; luckily, that approach often converted them into happy clients. Josh was well connected within the omnipotent assistant network of NYC, and at all times he covertly briefed the staff on my mood while handling me on a need-to-know basis.

When it didn't compromise the work of *And Baby*, I accepted—and on a good day, even adored—the chaotic, dynamic, comical way in which my office ran itself. Music was always blaring at work, and it wasn't unusual to witness Josh impersonating that chick in *Fame* through the office. Whenever he messed up in his duties, he melodramatically danced in and out of my doorframe, passionately singing, at the top of his lungs, to Mariah Carey or Madonna until the hilarity cracked my anger into chuckles, allowing him to feel forgiven. He took extraordinary pride in staying a step ahead of me. Josh was an exceptional assistant: effective, charming, and witty. He could have, without a doubt, sold ice to Eskimos if he wanted to.

Harris was altogether different. Big, androgynous, and amiable, he wore construction boots and a rugged lumberjack look, complete with a beard. As soon as he expressed contentment about getting my coffee, his very existence fueled an inexplicable rivalry in Josh, who picked on him incessantly—rarely to any avail. Harris hated the fact that Josh was so flamboyant; he felt it gave gay men like him a bad rep. Josh, meanwhile, detested the fact that Harris did his work without making a big fuss about it.

I had plucked Harris from an Italian restaurant X and I frequented in Brooklyn; he was a waiter with exceptional customer service but without a white-collar job under his belt. After *And Baby*, he went on to run global sales for a high-end perfume brand. Amazing. But back then, he was petrified at even the thought of placing a sales call, and he hyperventilated every time it came to closing a deal. Even so, he was a terrific writer and an all-around valuable asset to our team. And he was Jack's best pal, always there for her and attending to her every need.

In Jack, I once again had a nearly human, ever-present companion. She came to work with us whenever her schedule didn't indicate one Wagging Tail, a Manhattan doggy daycare in Tribeca. And did she ever love that place! Opening the passenger (her) door was sufficient when I pulled up to the curb; she needed no nudging to run across the wide sidewalk and into her bliss, most often without as much as a glance good-bye. Mind you, she took her leisure in style: even back in the early 2000s, Wagging Tail had web cameras with a live feed that enabled us to check on Jack throughout our work day, and they frequently took their own bus for daytrips to an Olympic-sized indoor swimming pool. Needless to say, Jack always got the Best Swimmer award. She also made it on television long before I did: she starred in MTV's dog show, *Kings & Queens of Manhattan*.

When she was not otherwise committed, Jackson, our very smart, laid-back people dog, had our entire office whipped. The offices of her two mothers bookended the vast space, and she claimed everything in between as her rightful realm. It seemed like whenever she wished for a stretch, any number of willing arms would send her ball sailing through the air. And she managed to take herself outside, down the elevator, whenever the need arose—often assisted by unaware button-pushers—and come back up of her own accord.

And here is what I witnessed every morning, same time: Josh would bring a muffin for his breakfast, which he had close to noon because he rarely showed up to work before eleven. Given his position, his phone was constantly ringing off the hook, so he would get his muffin nice and ready on his desk while looking for an opportune break to eat it. Before you knew it, one matter or another would get him to go out of his office—and he would come back to nothing but the wrapper. Josh would gasp, his arms would go up in the air, and then he would transcend disbelief and revel in rage: "Ja-a-ackso-o-on!!!"

This never failed to happen. Every day. I think Jack and I were the only ones who knew this was a game.

———

As a team, we had our beat outside as well as inside the office. For example, the P-Town Family Week, a landmark annual event for alternative families in Provincetown, Massachusetts, was huge for *And Baby*. Every August we rented the same beautiful home for a week. X and I would go on Monday, using the event as an opportunity to harness a holiday for ourselves; then the staff would join us on Thursday and help facilitate all of the weekend promotional activities that lasted through Sunday.

Every single night I, the ever-sober boss, would hear something like, "Shhhh . . ." *Bang, plunk, stomp.* "Shut up . . . Be quiet . . . !" My staff partied so hard they would fall walking *up* the stairs.

"It's okay, just give them a break, they are on holiday," X would tell me.

And then there was our office Christmas party, always around

December 15. There was a Christmas gift for everyone under the beautifully decorated tree they got to pick out every year.

"How about this one?" somebody new and reasonable would ask.

"Nah . . . Have to get the best, or she won't like it," the people who knew better would reply.

There wasn't much room for skimping. Our ceilings were thirty feet high, and I wasn't going to have some half-baked, balding tree. So ours were inevitably lush Douglas Furs, beautiful and at least $300.

We also joined the other business owners of the East Village in a toy drive every December, handing out presents to less fortunate local kids.

My staff would work for another week after the Christmas party before taking a two weeks' paid holiday that was not counted towards their annual leave. X and I, however, headed to our home in Pennsylvania right after the party. Outside of Christmas break, which I would often commence with a bad cold once my body dared relax, X and I were rarely in Milford together: we had opposite deadlines, hers with the art department and mine with my publisher duties and the sales department.

Myself, I fell into a bit of a rhythm with Pennsylvania: I would retreat there to approve the galley of each issue. The galley is the final collation of the magazine before it goes to print, with my approval as the publisher, and it was always the first time I read the upcoming issue of *And Baby* cover to cover. That's how I preferred it; that way, I could read it as a consumer rather than just as the publisher.

When it was galley time, I would try to leave the office on Thursday to beat the traffic and get to our little PA house in the late evening. Friday morning, I would pour myself a cup of coffee (or two), go through the issue with a fine-tooth comb, and deal with the office. Saturday would be more relaxed: for Jackson, diving in the river and running circles around the meadow, intermittent with stand-offs with bears, and for me, swimming, reading, meandering around town, and spending time in the paddock.

At some point I had bought an old ornery quarter horse and named him Reed. I had diverted him from his path to becoming hamburger in hopes of giving him a better life. He was a pain in the ass—a crabby ol' bastard who taught me a lot about trauma. He had been in love with his previous owner. Back when he was a cutting horse, she had been a young girl and they had caught cattle together. Upon turning seventeen, however, she had stopped riding and put him out to pasture. No more fame, no more togetherness, and one broken heart. For us, this meant that if I didn't come when Reed expected me, he would ignore me at best, or run me into fences at worst. But most Saturdays, we tried to spend time together.

On Sunday mornings, I would go to the local Unity church in Lafayette, New Jersey. The congregation was quite diverse, and our reverend was an amazing human being. Then I would either head back into the city, or, if I was staying until Monday morning, to that old Milford diner I loved so much.

I learned everything I knew about the town through that diner. And I learned an astounding amount about New York through my 10,000-sqare-foot office in Red Hook.

I loved that space. It was on the water. Classic. Beautiful. Timber picked up where the 1941 stone left off, and it boasted a magnificent, floor-to-ceiling fireplace. Did I mention the windows overlooked the Statue of Liberty?

Part of my negotiated condition for the very low rent of the raw, aging warehouse space I called home was that I would maintain it. Living up to that agreement kept me busy. Over the years I would install a few wood-burning stoves, go through four cords of wood every winter, fit out the space with clean-line furniture to celebrate its grit, and celebrate the clad-iron staircase that granted us access to the 360-degree-view rooftop.

Taking care of my space came with accepting responsibility for all the local guys who helped me. An informal but loyal team, they minded my parking spots, watched out for trespassers, and entertained my dog when she came downstairs to escape boredom. Over the years, I would come to view them as family.

———

Just as our lives were catching their rhythm, my broader New York family became the victim of one of modern time's most horrific tragedies: 9/11.

At the first blasts of the catastrophe, X and I went up to the roof of our office building. We stood there in a solemn line of over a dozen locals and watched as the second plane hit the World Trade Center.

The effect this tragic event had on me was to propel me into higher gear. I yearned to move faster with the impact of *And Baby* and to solidify my life. Now it felt more important than ever that we move on our engagement and marry—that we start a new chapter, in part for all those whose stories had been so cruelly cut short.

So we set our wedding day, and it would be mere two months out, November 17.

———

To plan the ceremony, I did what I believe any good boss would do: I put the wedding on my to-do list. My assistant treated the endeavor as a promotional event, and we went full steam ahead. We booked my family and friends travel from California, figured out our New York guest list, and picked out a venue. Our Unity church would host the ceremony.

The catering, the flowers, and all other necessary arrangements were completed within two months. X chose the color palette and designed the invitations. And even though my publicist came to the wedding, he came as a friend and we agreed to keep the wedding private: no cameras, no press.

Our guest list, however, was a bit shaky. 9/11 still had many of our California guests flight-skittish; most hadn't been to an airport since. (I, of course, didn't have the luxury of avoiding flights; work demanded it. In fact, I had been on a plane within two days of the tragedy.)

My mother stepped in and whipped most of the undecideds into shape.

On Thursday, November 15, three minivans picked up our guests from JFK and brought them to 7A in the East Village, my favorite diner in NYC, where they all shared breakfast before heading to Pennsylvania. The local bed-and-breakfast became their home for the next four days. X and I, just the two of us, stayed in our house.

The day was everything I had hoped it would be. I was getting the winter wedding I had always wanted, and it was rather intimate, around sixty people. The day was unbelievably gorgeous: clear, crisp, and sprinkled with snow. The décor was elegant. For catering, we hired Hollywood Caterers, a firm I had repeatedly used for my clients' events, and in addition to putting on a spectacular banquet, they made us an exquisite gift: for desert, each person received a hand-blown chocolate dessert, magnificent in its presentation and out-of-this-world delicious.

Many of my business associates attended, and this intensified my joy, as I was surrounded by the perfect fusion of everything I held dear in my life: my bride, our families, our dear friends, and the people who had made possible my ambitious work in the world.

Some of my colleagues later pointed out how shocked they were to see me cry, so happy, as we said our vows during the ceremony. X, in contrast, stayed stoic through the entire event. In hindsight, I wonder if she was merely going through the motions, trying not to rock the boat of what we had set in place. All I can know for sure is that it was one of the best days of my life.

The next day, I was enjoying some quiet time with my friends when one of them blurted out, "Dude! Your mother really had your back yesterday, the way you wouldn't believe!"

My mother doesn't take much flak and can be quite terrifying once she starts speaking her mind.

"Are you friggin' kidding me?" I said, imagining the scene. "What the heck did she do!?"

I found and cornered my mom, but she brushed off my question.

"I don't want to talk about it," she said. "It's none of your damn business, anyway; I took care of it."

So my investigation took me back to my friends and indicated that whatever had happened, X's parents were involved.

Given the earlier events that had revealed their staunch views about our "lifestyle choices," X had deliberated whether to invite her parents to the wedding at all, but I had encouraged her to include them. "They are still your parents," I had insisted. So we had covered the costs of them coming, and, in return, I discovered, they had brought their homophobia to my very wedding.

X's mother, seated at the family table, allegedly went around asking many guests whether they thought it was alright, acceptable, to hold such a ceremony. Until my mother got hold of her, that is.

"How dare you do this today?" my mom demanded. "What you said back *then*, she will never forgive you for it; she will respect you, but never forgive. Shame on you that you lost her as a daughter. She adored you; she did and would have always done anything for you. And yet here you are, at her wedding, and she is treating you like royalty. How dare you!?"

I was told that my ex-mother-in-law had no response and just lowered her head.

———

People often wonder what will change once they are married, especially if they have been living with their partner for a while. For me, the most significant change was testifying to each other and to the LGBT community of our commitment to one another and intentions to build a family together.

What didn't change materially was our daily life. We continued to work very hard, enjoy Italian food and play with Jackson together, and do pretty much everything else apart. Over time, we seemed to allow the pressure and fatigue to push out any intimate time together; even our dinners were no longer a point of connection, as the magazine seemed to be the only topic we shared interest in. Our interactions became more and more fleeting and businesslike, prosaic and focused solely on tending to our household issues, caring for Jack, and planning our workweeks and trips to Pennsylvania.

Together, we were never ones to goof around. If my friends or my sister were around, I could count on cracking up throughout the day; in fact, I would do well to plan on laughing until my tummy hurt, and on staying up too late doing so. But X and I did not do that. We lived side by side, our life equable and lowkey, and I grew to enjoy what we did have.

In the beginning, when we came to the Pennsylvania house, we would lie around, watch TV, and rest together. But even those experiences dissipated over time. We got things done, took care of bills, and appeared all buttoned up externally. But our relationship wasn't warm; it felt respectful, polite, functional, and lonely. It wasn't how I would have wished my marriage to feel, but I had accepted who X was and who we were together. I wonder if at some point, having tried what she could, she just gave up on me.

I was becoming more and more aware that X expected things—especially my schedule—to change. That she had hoped

I would stop pursuing all those things outside the realm of what she perceived to be normal family life once we got married. She may have assumed I would be taking more time off work. But if anything, the *And Baby* commitment was getting more intense.

X was asking for more time together; to make it happen, I asked my assistant for scheduling help. Why? Because on many occasions I had found myself un-committing to X because of a prior obligation in the diary that he controlled.

X crucified me for it.

"How dare you make me go through your assistant!?" she confronted me angrily.

By this point in our relationship, my efforts to make things better only seemed to make them worse. This encounter was no different.

To compound matters, our relationship had never been fueled by communication. In fact, X didn't speak to me much at all. It wasn't until the tirades, arguments, and court statements during the dissolution of our relationship that I learned what she claimed to have felt and thought throughout our life together.

I don't blame her for being angry with me; she is entitled to that. I was a lousy partner—self-absorbed, at times abrasive, always a workaholic. I assumed that my aspirations in life were intuitively and commonly shared by many, if not all. Who wouldn't want to have a life that had both the seclusion of a weekend getaway and the glamour of celebrity outings? Who wouldn't want to have staff at the house to alleviate the household burdens and make more time for life? Who wouldn't want to contribute to their cause well enough to attract recognition?

But this is not the story of "us," nor is it X's story. I am quite sure that the latter would be altogether different. I am no doubt the "bad guy" in her story; hey, I even play that role in my own story at times. But in my story, I also never once considered that the life I was building wasn't the one X wanted.

CHAPTER 4:
YEAH, BABIES!

BOND: something that binds, fastens, confines, or holds together; a covenant.

Even as we both adjusted our expectations of our marriage, whether we would have children together was never in question. We would occasionally get some flak in the press: the couple behind the first alternative parenting magazine in the country was "yet to have children of their own." However, the day-to-day running of the magazine was taking all of our time, focus, and energy.

I remember distinctly the day we decided to make our family a reality.

We were headed home to our little rooftop apartment in Brooklyn. It was a beautiful day: the air was crisp and clean; the street was abuzz with people walking, buying groceries, chatting, and going about their business. A typical day in the neighborhood.

As we pulled up to a stop sign, we saw a young couple pushing a baby carriage. They were a beautiful family—stunning mom, handsome dad, and a gorgeous baby—and all three were floating, smiling, harmonious. Time just seemed to slow down; it was the weirdest, most surreal experience.

X looked over at me and said, "I am ready to start our family."

The look in her eyes was undeniable; I knew better than to negotiate on this one. Inside, though, my heart skipped a beat. I was excited, of course; this was what I had been dreaming about. But the excitement was shadowed by worry.

The magazine remained demanding. We were already being heralded as a success story, but our road was far from traveled, and many shortcuts traditional publications could take for granted didn't exist for us—a difference that at times threatened our survival. I took every challenge on the chin and had yet to even contemplate defeat coming within blocks of my creation. However, keeping things afloat took nearly all of my time, energy, tenacity, and care. How would I make sure there was enough for everyone, including, now, a baby?

Then again, they say there is never a "perfect time" to start a family, and on principle, I really wanted one. It had always felt like a part of the plan for us, and my wife was ready. So I opted for children, however imperfect the timing.

———

One morning, I called a meeting and informed our staff that we were going to get pregnant and that we had chosen California Cryobank in Los Angeles, which was one of *And Baby*'s clients at the time.

"OMG!"

"You've got to be kidding!"

"Finally!"

"SO happy for you guys, YAY!"

The staff were thrilled; in fact, for a week, all of them appeared to devote every working moment to vetting, comparing, pitching, and otherwise growing personally vested in the many qualified donors on Cryobank's website. Although I was elated by their support and grateful for the help, we still had a magazine to run. So I finally had to pull rank and end the craziness.

"You have no idea how much we appreciate your excitement and support," I said when I took the floor at the following Monday's production meeting. "However, we have subscribers, sponsors, our community. So the new and non-negotiable mandate is that no donor lookups are to occur during business hours."

The resolution was noted on the agenda, and the staff, begrudgingly and with long faces, obliged.

───────

As the weeks went on, X and I dug deep into planning our family: short-listing doctors, dealing with our healthcare provider, and making every one of the million decisions befitting such a life-changing endeavor. The one decision that I will always be grateful for is that X and I agreed to choose an "open" donor, which allows the child to look up his or her father upon turning eighteen. We concurred that this decision should be up to our child and not us.

Even though I was the CEO and majority shareholder of *And Baby*, and of course honored domestic partnerships within the company, X and I had to have two separate healthcare policies because—you guessed it—our healthcare provider did not yet recognize domestic partnerships. Ironic, but true.

There are many procedures to choose from when going along the "making a baby" track. The original intention was that the doctors would do an egg extraction from me, fertilize it outside the womb, and implant it in X, who would carry and deliver the concoction. I was thirty-seven years old; X was thirty-three. If we were going to do this, now was the time. My eggs weren't getting any younger! This added another level of complexity to our already-intricate baby-making process.

Our healthcare provider gave us our OB/GYN. He in turn

suggested two world-renowned doctors who had started the insemination program at Columbia University, which boasted an impressive 96 percent success rate in pregnancies for women over forty. The typical overachieving New Yorkers, they were perfect. Our minds were made up; these would be our guys.

Unlike X, I wasn't passionate about experiencing pregnancy itself. As a matter of fact, I can only recall one time, for about a week, when my biological clock was screaming at me, "You must have a baby!" I was about twenty-six at the time, and I just kept saying to myself, "Not now, not now." And the feeling passed—whew!—never to return again. My body was in the clear. And lucky for me, I was a lesbian, so I never had to come to terms with, "This is your duty as a wife." I was a wife, of course, but I was a different kind—the kind that didn't get pregnant.

My publicist was based in LA, and I was there at least once a month for clients, guest appearances on radio and talk shows, all the typical publisher and public relations stuff that comes with running a national magazine. The California Cryobank clinic was among the *And Baby* advertisers I would be meeting with, but for the next trip, I made room in my diary for something more personal in addition to a regular client-relations visit.

I met with the bank's executive director. She explained to me how stringent the donor selection process was, and we laughed together when she remarked that she knew more about the donors' medical histories than about her own husband's.

As I toured the facility and the lab, I noticed that one room in particular was very quiet. Scientists in white lab coats looked quite busy, but there was an air of serenity in the space. There were large vats with millions of small vials and what appeared to be dry ice emanating from them. I, of course, couldn't help myself and blurted out, "Oh my god . . . they are so cute—and TINY!"

The scientists broke out in laughter; serenity gave way to a majestic, unforgettable sense of possibility for our family.

Now, we had to home in on the donor. One night I was in my office after the staff had gone home for the day, and X was in hers across the floor. She walked over and through my doorway. "I have found the perfect donor."

And that he was: tall, healthy, intelligent, athletic. It was decided.

We didn't actually do the insemination for quite a few more months because the magazine was going gangbusters. I was in negotiation with the first LGBT television network to host and executive produce the first-ever alternative parenting TV series on Time Warner/Cable. The scenario where my eggs were fertilized started to become less and less plausible.

"I have to put up with you as it is. If you let them shoot hormones into your ass every week, I quit!"

This ultimatum came from my assistant, Josh. I guess it was no secret that I was already a handful to deal with, sans additional hormones. Neither was it a surprise that my incredibly competent, dramatic assistant chose the style of Shakespearean tragedy to make the point.

So, by popular—vocal, assertive, non-negotiable—demand, my eggs were off the hook; it was to be all X, in the meticulous hands of our overqualified doctors.

With all the hustle-bustle and both of us working full-time-plus, our doctors completely handled the process; we just showed up for the check-ups, the hormone shots, and the measurements.

The day finally came for our scheduled insemination. We agreed to meet at the doctors' office. I had been in back-to-back meetings, and of course there was tons of traffic, so I was running late. When I finally rushed into the room, X was ready to go, stirrups and all. I felt so bad—and she didn't look happy. I didn't blame her; of all the days to be late, this was a bad one.

Still trying to catch my breath, I sat on the low stool next to the doctor; he passed me the syringe and I pushed, the energy of the day still pulsating through my veins. The missing piece of the DNA rushed along a tube—*Excessively long*, I thought—and into our lives.

"Slow down . . . slow down . . ." the doctor said, indicating his preferred pace to me with his voice. Despite the uncontestable medical presence, it was a beautiful, truly awe-some moment.

———

A few weeks after the insemination took place, X and I were walking in Manhattan on a busy Saturday afternoon. We were waiting for the traffic light to cross the street when she grabbed my arm and told me that we were pregnant. I had heard that some women know these things; I had even heard some state that they knew in the moment, during sex, that they had conceived. We just happened to find out when standing on the corner of Fifth Avenue. Just like that, on the first attempt, we were a family.

After the appropriate amount of time passed, we announced to our world that we were expecting. All were thrilled. But we forgot a very influential individual.

"I think Jackson is mad at me," X said one day.

"Why?" I asked, oblivious.

"I think because I'm pregnant."

Dismissive of the possibility of such an astute reaction from Jack, I looked at her where she was lying on the ground a couple of yards away, and guess what . . . she got up, turned around, and lay back down—with her back to us!

That's when I realized: *We never told Dog!*

So we sat her down and told her everything.

Over the course of the next few months, we went through the complicated, punctuated, intrusive, and exhilarating process of sonograms, ultrasounds, checks-to-this, and swabs-to-that. For a brief moment the doctors thought we might be having triplets . . . and I about had a heart attack. However, when it came to that appointment when your heart gets to flutter because you hear the babies, there were only two heartbeats. Twins. Fraternal. Separate sacks.

"Twins!?" the doctor that had guided me during our insemination later chimed in. "I told you that you were going too fast! All your fault!"

The next sonogram suggested a boy and a girl, and we went on that belief for a few months until the new sonogram outperformed the previous one.

"I see two girls," the doctor said quietly. I never thought I'd have girls, but instantaneously that was the most natural news we could have gotten.

Right around that time, on December 6, 2002, Oprah Winfrey, Nelson Mandela, and the local Ministry of Education broke ground for the Oprah Winfrey Leadership Academy for Girls in South Africa. It was an amazing venture, and I birthed a dream to feature Oprah on the cover of *And Baby*.

"Please, find me some way, any way, to get to Oprah's camp," I told my New York publicist. Through the publicist network, we were lucky to get the direct number for Gail King, Oprah's lifetime best friend and now the residing editor-at-large of *O Magazine*.

I called her and told her who I was.

"Hey, girl!" Gail responded.

I explained what *And Baby* was about, and the honor I was hoping for.

"I got you," she said. "Her schedule is usually filled up at least a year in advance, but send me the information and I will see what we can do."

I sent her a package through Bloom, my favorite florist in New York—a package that I hoped expressed my respect and appreciation, not just conveyed the opportunity. It was an exquisite, foot-high tree sprinkled with intricate rose blossoms, all set in a marvelous pot. Just the most gorgeous thing; I could not pass it up.

Several days passed, and then Josh screamed into my office, "Holy shit! Gail King is on the phone for you!"

"Hey, girl!" There was her inviting voice again. "The gift you sent is beautiful, thank you so much." I was holding my breath for a miracle. "Unfortunately, like I said, Oprah is booked about sixteen months out at the moment, and there isn't wiggle room. But I wanted to call you and thank you myself. We commend what you are doing, please keep at it."

After I hung up, I addressed the small crowd of staff that had gravitated toward the magnitude of that call. "That is how one should always behave," I told them. "Gracious and respectful, no matter how successful one is."

I have never measured success or influence by the amount of money one has. I am not one to admire celebrity, or to grant somebody power over me or my work just because he or she is the one holding the checkbook. For me, success is the measure of one's legacy, the number of lives one touches and elevates to the next level.

"I must instill this lesson in my daughters," I added to myself, looking forward to a day when I would share this story with them.

———

As we prepared for our daughters' arrival, our rooftop apartment was deemed inadequate. I went on a search for a more spacious abode. The lucky townhouse that was to be our next home got a major makeover: I used the time in the lead-up to the babies' arrival to make two bedrooms and a bath out of the open-plan basement. The beautiful iron spiral staircase made complete child-proofing impossible, but some creative workarounds did get put in place before we moved in.

But why, with all this spare energy, stop at one remodel when you can do two? So our Pennsylvania house also got some action: we received a gift of two beautiful, handmade furniture sets, and we remodeled the room we planned to use as a nursery.

Having kids showed us just how much *And Baby*'s clients valued our work, because generous, thoughtful, and timely gifts accompanied us throughout the girls' early childhood. The girls were possibly the best-known twins within the LGBT community, and it celebrated them generously.

X was a pro at the pregnancy thing: she stayed really healthy, did super well, and "baked them," as we used to say, beyond the thirty-four weeks that are considered to be full term for twins. It was no surprise, then—and X has my eternal gratitude for this—that both girls were off-the-charts healthy (and have continued on this overachieving path since).

The "Letter from the Publisher" in the May/June 2003 issue of *And Baby Magazine* featured my journal entry from the day after the grand celebration that was the birth of our children.

It's 1:30 A.M. I have just arrived at home. As I pour myself a cup of tea, my mind begins to recall the events of this glorious day. At 6:19 and 6:20 P.M. (one minute apart) our daughters entered the world. Juliette came first, at 6.2 pounds and 19 inches. Alyssa followed at 6.3 pounds, 19 ¼ inches.

This is how the day unfolded. It started like any other busy day. At the office by 8 A.M., sifting through countless messages, responding to emails and preparing for departmental meetings—the usual magazine stuff, the busy and hurried life of a publisher. Boy, was I soon to find out that this day would be one of the most important days of my life—a day that would change my life forever.

Around 11 A.M., I stopped by my wife's office. As usual, she looked beautiful and radiant, but something seemed different. Her eyes were a vibrant green and her energy level seemed higher than it had been in the last few months. We chatted briefly about the excitement of Friday (our scheduled C-section date: both babies were breached). But to our surprise, Alyssa and Juliette had other plans.

Around lunchtime, a meeting I was attending was cut short by the news that X's water had broken. My heart began racing. A nervous energy consumed me. X, on the other hand, was calm, collected, and ready to go to the hospital. As we drove through Manhattan (to my amazement, with no traffic) I must have asked X a million times "Are you okay?"

When we arrived at the hospital, everything proceeded like clockwork. I double-parked, turned my hazards on (something else unheard of in Manhattan) and whisked her up to the labor room. As we prepared for delivery, I had this sense of joy in my heart that could only be expressed through tears. This was the moment we had been waiting for, planned for, dreamed of.

As the surgery began, the radio pumped out U2's "In the Name of Love," and just a short while later our baby girls were born. Happy, healthy, and content. As I looked in my wife's eyes, I was (as the Buddhists say) in a state of Nirvana. X: Beautiful, wise, brave, gentle being, I honor and love you to the depth of my soul. To my girls: You are incredible, perfect beings of God and I am honored and blessed to be your mother.

Thank you to our readers for allowing me to share my experience with you. Thank you for your words of encouragement, your email, and congratulatory letters. Thank you for supporting and believing in And Baby Magazine. *We believe that having children is a cherished human right, and that all children deserve a family who loves them. Now more than ever, I know that we are right.*

With gratitude,
Michelle Darné

———

In the operating room, the dozen medical staff were dancing and bobbing their heads to the beat when our doctor cracked his knuckles and said, "Let's do this!"—but nothing could have prepared me for the overwhelming, unconditional love I felt for Juliette and Alyssa from their first moment in this world.

My best friend and sister—and an expert mother of two healthy, well-adjusted children—came from California to be with us. Not counting our wonderful, happy, bald doctor, she was the first to hold the babies. I was elated for all of us.

As I held my babies, something changed and at the same time firmly placed my heart in a state ever-present in human history: I just knew, in a place deeper than words or emotion, that I now had a new and greater purpose to fulfill—that my life had just become more significant.

The babies were perfect, and in some cosmic way, they had chosen me to be their parent. As if witnessing myself rather than deliberating over it, I solemnly accepted this honor and vowed to do and sacrifice anything for them. Little did I know that these thoughts were truly prophetic.

X started running a fever after delivery and had to stay in

the hospital for four days. I was hustling between the hospital and the office numerous times through the day. The C-section we had scheduled was supposed to take place in mid-April, almost a week away, and my intention had been to take an entire month off to be with my family. The babies, of course, came early, which meant that my efforts to clear everything out at work had to catch up.

Then came the first twenty-four hours of them being home. My sister, kind, compassionate woman that she is, went with me to pick up the family and even offered to stay the night.

"No problem," I said. "I GOT THIS—go get some sleep."

Mind you, X had to stay in bed and I had not the slightest clue what I was doing.

Needless to say, when my sister came back at 7:00 a.m., we were a sight: I still had on my white robe (idiot), covered in puke, and both me and the babies were exhausted because none of us had slept all night. They had screamed, and screamed, and screamed . . . I had cuddled them, walked with them, and rocked (spastically, toward the morning) them simultaneously in their cribs, all to no avail.

We were already sleep deprived after ten days into being the novice parents of twins when my controller called to inform me that the magazine's scheduled investment transfer had not arrived. I told her we'd be fine, to use our credit line and to wait for it to show up. It never did. And neither did two more scheduled installments.

I learned later that my main investor, by then a close friend and our children's godfather, had, against my advice and that of others, overextended himself on his new high-risk venture, hedging *And Baby*'s funds and unwittingly pulling the rug from underneath it. With those funds, we had been on schedule to break even that year. Instead, here I was, going back to work within two weeks, torn between wanting to be with and take care of my family and needing to do everything in my power, as inconspicuously as possible, to keep our company from collapsing.

During that time, I would get to the office before 7:00 a.m. and come home by 6:00 p.m. to bathe the girls and put them to bed before going back at 8:00 p.m. for a second shift at the office. For a while, this was the "witching hour," as the babies had colic and just screamed, at the top of their lungs, for the straight two hours that I was home. I could not have been more grateful to have no neighbors at the time.

Given our exhaustion, the crisis at the magazine was putting an enormous strain on my marriage. A couple of times, X yelled at me, "I am the only one up all night with the babies!" Given that it was not her habit to tell me what she needed, or to look for a solution with me, that would be all the cue I got to figure it out. We needed the rest, so, even though we could not afford it, I found a night nurse. And oh, my, was that the wisest decision I could have made!

I couldn't believe my eyes when, within minutes of the nurse's arrival, the babies were bathed, blissfully sucking on binkies, and watching TV with her on the couch. That's when I knew that babies know things. Things you don't always want them to know—like, for example, when your immediate ability to care for their precious selves needs to catch up to their standards. We had interviewed nannies before the babies were born but ended up activating those arrangements more to save our sanity than as part of the calm, planned process we had envisioned. The extra beautiful thing was that our hardworking nanny was Creole, from Haiti, so she spoke French. The kids could grow up bilingual!

I was hoping that hiring the night nurse would help both of us, as well as counter the resentment that X seemed to be building toward me. However, it only seemed to make things worse. Perhaps she expected me to invisibly do everything that needed to be done at work, bring home the bacon, and also be available, energized, and rested so I could stay up all night with the children. I do not know. But I felt mocked for every step I took, regardless of its overwhelming cost, to address the challenges she indicated needed solving.

On a really bad day, even the ever-so-predictable would get to me, like when I was taken for a nanny because what other business would I, a scrappy little brown woman with a pencil in her hair, have walking two picture-perfect white children?

And Baby was in the red. I had briefed the staff on our struggles and made it clear that I would not hold it against anybody who wished, in the face of likely instability, to leave. Everybody stayed. Salaries were delayed at times, but we were all pulling together.

Even while strapped, *And Baby* survived for about six months on revenue from sales, favors, and its credit line. By November, however, we were in crisis and headed into an emergency meeting. It was 7:00 p.m. on a Friday night, so all the staff was gone, and it was my attorneys and accountants who were filling the conference room.

"Michelle, on Monday you have to lay everybody off," they told me. "It is the only way."

"But I can't do that," I protested. "They put their trust in me; they are family. And holidays are coming up. I have done this before, and I will do this again; I will raise the money."

"Sounds like a Joan of Arc maneuver. You don't have to put this on yourself. We advise you not to do this."

Monday came and went without anybody getting laid off. One of the worst business decisions I have ever made. This book serves in part as a memorial to the many bad choices I made trying to care for my family. By refusing to cut its losses, I sentenced *And Baby* to spiraling deeper into the red, with no end in sight.

The only silver lining was the girls. The nanny would bring them by the office, and they would instantly become the soul of the place, handed from staff member to staff member, adored, loved up, and allowed on keyboards, in cupboards, and in meetings. Jackson would babysit, so I taught her a game she perfected: she would lie on the floor several feet away from the babies and push the beach ball to one, and then to the other. The kids would squeal in excitement and push the ball back to Jack, who could do this over, and over, and over again.

It was amazing to witness how by only five months of age, the girls were distinct people, their personalities and temperaments coming through loud and clear—and independent from each other. This was marvelously apparent at their Christening: Juliette was laughing the entire time, the rose petals were an absolute hit with her, and she thought the entire experience was the greatest thing. Alyssa, meanwhile, was apprehensive and stunned, with huge blue deer-in-the-headlights eyes and a face begging the question, "Why would you do this to me?"

When left to their own devices, Alyssa would climb up and stand on top of Juliette—just the way she did in the womb. Alyssa was driven toward anything she could physically do. She ran before she walked and didn't talk until way after her sister (because why bother, right?). Juliette, in contrast, was a communicator from birth. She didn't see the point in walking as much as in talking and was a mouthpiece for her sister from the moment she could speak.

Within several months of her arrival in the world, Juliette had her own (toy) phone. And she used it masterfully, stepping out to take calls and always introducing herself.

A friend of mine told me one day, "Hey, by the way, your daughter called."

"What?!?" The girls were barely a year old. But frankly, the immediate shock quickly gave way to a sense of acceptance. The toy phone would no longer do, but pushing buttons on my work phone would do just fine!

We had our favorite games together—often involving Jackson, of course. With Alyssa, we would sing "Rock Star Baby"; I would start, and she would add, "yeah . . . yeah!" and toss her blond curls about.

Juliette would often chase me with an open mouth for a kiss; she was very affectionate and cuddly. We'd dance together. From the beginning she had this free spirit. She was relaxed, intelligent, and found everything just so funny.

When they were about eight months old, a friend of ours came over. We were prepping lunch in the kitchen and the girls were in their high chairs, banging their plates and forks in energetic anticipation. I turned to them and said, "What do we do when we get stressed?"

Juliette immediately folded her tiny hands into prayer position and made the *Om* sound. Alyssa joined in.

Our friend's jaw dropped. "Are they doing what I think they are doing?!"

The babies, so different, so ours, blew my mind all the time.

———

While our daughters' world was perfect, ours was cracking like the concrete-clad playgrounds that New Yorkers call "parks." X was growing more and more frustrated. She had expressed multiple times, to me and to others, that she had never wanted to live in New York, let alone raise a child there—and now there were two. Even the inability to bring the double stroller through the doors was difficult for her to ignore. And increasingly, any attempt on my part to help appeared to only make matters worse. One day she fired the nanny, and not longer after, we left New York.

We had had a discussion about what would be best and decided that moving X and the girls, then fourteen months old, to California was it. Out of "harm's way" of my unabated stress, and somewhere they could live in a nice house with a lawn and other benefits of nonurban living.

My next business trip to San Francisco, on May 16, 2004, was for an interview with the *San Francisco Chronicle*, which had asked to do a feature story on me: a Bay Area girl redefines parenting from New York and returns to give back to her roots. The photo for that story portrays a grounded, openhearted woman energized by her work. But during the photo shoot I felt like such a fraud, imprisoned within a personal brand at work. I didn't feel victorious. *And Baby*'s very important work was being threatened by nothing more than cash flow constraints, I wasn't ready to be back in California, and I was mourning the loss of the already sparse time I had with my girls. Thus, even as the photographer counted down, "Three . . . two . . . one!" that smile was harder and harder to hold.

After the challenging interview I went to see my sister in Concord, and I saw that the house right across the street from her was up for rent. The moment I told X, she asked, "Did you take it?"—and we immediately did, without ever setting foot inside.

My parents and siblings, most of whom had not even had a chance to meet the only twins of our whole family, were thrilled.

However unusual our life was by many measures, all parents are made equal when it comes to taking their fourteen-month-olds on a cross-country flight. The worst, longest six-hour flight of my life took place on Memorial Day weekend 2004. With hyper-mobile, busy toddlers who did not understand why they could not make the entire plane their playground, and why it was not funny to torture the passengers in the row in front of us through incessant foot stabbings, it was a humbling journey. Never again would I feel justified in snapping at the frazzled parents of that baby who has cried for the entire duration of the flight when they hoped she would sleep through it. Exhausted, we were marking this new chapter of our lives with sweat, tears, and cracker crumbs all the way to San Francisco.

CHAPTER 5:

BICOASTAL, AGAIN

COMPROMISE: a settlement of differences by mutual concessions; an agreement reached by adjustment of conflicting or opposing claims, principles, etc., by reciprocal modification of demands.

The Oakland Airport is a bit of a cornerstone place for me, perhaps because it became one of the first places where I safely felt adult independence when I started flying on my own for traveling soccer. The arrivals terminal spit us—me, X, and the babies—out into the huggy-kissy arms of my parents and sister. Later they told me that what I felt as drained and messy looked more like something the cat had dragged in: my hair was disheveled; my gaze had that beyond-panicked, distant expression; and my clothes looked as if they'd been chewed, thoroughly, within a mouthful of baby snacks. Definitely not the smooth executive traveler I always claimed to be.

A few well-trotted on-ramps, exits, and turns, and we arrived at our new home, where my family had fashioned an unthinkable present: they had unloaded the moving truck and set up our entire house. The furniture was all in place, polished and just right. The bed and cribs were made with fresh linens, beckoning. The fridge was stocked with groceries, all the dishes were put away for a functional kitchen, and a delicious dinner was on the table. They had worked tirelessly for the previous forty-eight hours.

I had no idea they had planned on doing this and had braced myself for stuffing the exhaustion inside for days so I could set up the house. X seemed as grateful as I was. I wanted to cry, but I just hugged them all.

My mother was beyond excited to introduce the babies to their new home, put together with such expectant love. She took them outside, stripped them down to their diapers—it was a scorching hundred-degree day—scouted out some shade in the backyard, and put them down on the grass.

"Here you are, how is that? Nice and soft."

Their reaction countered all of our expectations: they started screeching and pulling their little chubby feet up, away from the ground. They had never encountered grass before! Everybody burst out laughing, of course, and gently guided their journey of discovery.

In that moment, I actually felt we had made the right choice. Every kid needs grass, and it was all going to be okay.

Before long, the girls were asleep, cozy and peaceful, in the cribs in their new bedroom. X, too, had called it a night.

I, on the other hand, couldn't sleep. I took myself outside, to the table in the backyard. But for the crickets, it was quiet. I smoked a cigarette, mused on my day, and sorted out my feelings about all that life might have in store for me.

I had not planned on returning to the Bay Area for quite some time, if ever. Don't get me wrong: I loved San Francisco and was open to living there again. But then X insisted that we rent the house near my sister, and now here we were, in the suburbs of the East Bay, about forty-five minutes and many social eons away from the actual city. And much closer to where I grew up.

I knew that here, the world of my amazing, unstoppable little girls, both of them named after courageous revolutionaries, would be cut down to size—encroached upon by generations of narrow-mindedness that saw no need for the arts or international news because their world barely extended beyond East Bay, retail sales, and domestic drama.

What I am writing may be perceived as judgmental or ungrateful. If you asked my girls today, "What does Mama say it means to be so talented and blessed?" they would tell you, though perhaps rolling their eyes a little at the chore of having to repeat it, "It means that we have a lot of responsibility to the world."

I do not judge the people whose worlds are small. I simply feel the duty to live in the world as I know it: vast, complicated, devastated by avoidable suffering, capable of producing extraordinary human miracles, and in need of courage, innovation, and compassion.

Some people may not even remember the stupid things they did in their early twenties, but it was clear to me then that drugs, alcohol, and I could come together only in devastation and ultimately death. In the anguish of my rock bottom, I made a contract with the Universe: If you help me get clean and stay clean, I will give my whole life to fulfilling your purpose; to fighting injustice, to speaking for those without a voice, and to elevating the disenfranchised into a life of wholeness. I am thirty years into discovering how to best live out that mandate.

An organization that supports addicts puts a lot of value on coalescing one's circumstances so that they are conducive to staying clean. Thus, I have always felt the responsibility to create for myself the circumstances that will enable me to fulfill my contract.

And Baby, my most significant creation under that contract so far, was collapsing, but I felt that for X, my efforts to save it or to at least soften the landing for our family, the staff, and the investors were a foregone conclusion of my dismal performance as a spouse and a mother. I even felt as if X was meticulously undoing what I had achieved and placing me right back where I started. That night, as I sat in our new backyard, I felt profound failure and humiliation for having moved not an inch.

———

I had to go back to NYC within a week, and that marked my transition to the new normal. I would once again be bicoastal, but with quite a stark contrast to the way I had lived that lifestyle the last time around. X and I would live separate lives. Her behavior around the home and toward me would start to resemble that of a single mom. And I would feel written off, trapped, and even set up into a scenario that appeared to be my only option but was wrong on all levels.

During that time, I took Sunday morning flights from Oakland to JFK, New York, got to bed by 10:00 p.m., and was at the office around 7:00 a.m. on Monday morning. This schedule helped me not miss a beat at the office—no jet lag or losing my mind.

In New York, I was starting a TV show. I had always envisioned that once *And Baby* built a following, I would regurgitate its content on all forms of media; as I used to say, "If the dogs eat the dog food . . ." This vision was big, given that I had never been on television before, but somehow I knew that was the brand's future. So when a TV network approached me to produce *And Baby* under the banner of *Here Family*, it felt like a perfect move all around: a solid step in my career, a logical transition for the magazine's readership, and a way to mask the underlying drama unfolding in my personal life.

I had struck a historic three-pronged deal with the network in which I was paid as the executive producer, since we were effectively parlaying into television the magazine I was publishing; the talent, which in this case was the industry term for my role as host; and as a business development executive, because I was to retain a nifty percentage of all sponsorship brought to the table. These were days long before cross-platform advertising packages. All media was segregated, so the contacts I dealt with for the magazine were not in a position to negotiate a deal that would feature their brand across print, TV, and radio. But I knew it could be done, not to mention that it simply made sense. Once again, I was doing my laborious bit of paving the way to the future.

We carved out a television studio in our 10,000-square-foot Redhook office, and on shooting days I would only emerge out of my apartment on the other side of the space when it was time to start hair and makeup.

Yes, that's right—I started living at the office. To afford the California home, I needed to let go of our townhouse. I spoke openly with my office landlord, who had become a friend and a business partner, to check how he felt about Jack and I staying in the office during our New York stints. Nobody else was living in the building, and it was zoned commercial, but he said he was okay with the arrangement as long as I kept it on the down-low.

After a few months, X called for Jackson. "The kids really miss the dog," she told me.

I sent her, and felt better that the kids were more protected, even though I wasn't home.

But apart from that, I was grieving.

It was no longer me and Jack. It was just me, living in an unfinished, not-yet-suitable-for-living office space and throwing myself under the weight of my crumbling magazine. Like a shadow world, my business life had been collapsing, even with the TV deal. After our investor had shortchanged *And Baby* by $750,000 across three scheduled installments, I had stopped playing softball and soccer to devote every second to capital raising. My attorney, Chris, and I initiated a frenzy of investment meetings, and we traversed the entire Eastern seaboard to drum up funds. That is when I perfected my "game face"; no matter how broken I felt inside, I would put my makeup on, even if in the car, and stave off despair for just long enough to elevate the issues of the LGBT community and to inspire my audience. Sometimes these efforts garnered a standing ovation, but even so they ultimately generated only inadequate dribbles of the funds we needed so desperately.

We managed to scrape up $150,000-odd through these meetings, but *And Baby Magazine* was breathing its last. I had to lay off all but three of my staff and pronounce *And Baby* time of death to my distributor.

"Don't rack me this month," I informed him.

"Got it." He kindly didn't ask for details.

I walked away—and into a taste of employee betrayal. I had engaged a new creative director to replace X after the babies were born, but after we lost our funding, I could no longer afford her on staff. Not wanting to let her down and still needing her expertise, I offered to pay her as a contractor if she still wanted the work. Which she did, and was grateful—until the work ran out, at which point she turned me into the Labor Board for evading employer responsibility.

I knew they had the grounds to charge me, but I never would have expected this person to stab me in the back simply because I was no longer doing for her what she wanted me to. In the end, I had to pay thousands of dollars in back taxes and fork out her unemployment for nearly two years.

On the weekends, attempting to escape my grief, I merely transported it to Pennsylvania. My country sanctuary stood a reminder of everything that didn't eventuate, until I sold it about five-six months after the family moved to California.

We had never intended to sell the Pennsylvania house; it was going to stay in the family. But by this point X didn't want anything to do with her former birthday present. It had become a burden, and, besides, we needed the money. The proceeds took care of outstanding bills and then some, so my family was again enjoying a period of relative stability and quiet.

I had vetted the buyers carefully and finally consented to sell to an elderly couple that seemed like they would enjoy and cherish the place. Many years later, in 2013, I went back only to find no remnants of the house I had known. After a few passes I had to accept that the grand structure in front of me in the clearing had been my property. I guess people really aren't always what they seem. The house had been leveled; the grand trees that used to line my driveway had been razed. That house must have been more in concert with my marriage than I ever thought.

My New York social circle had shrunk substantially by this point. It is a counterintuitive phenomenon that many public people apparently experience: as the outward life of my public persona got more visible, I craved to make the rest of my life more private. Surprisingly (even to me), I grew introverted and protective.

These tendencies increased to new heights when our children were born and immediately became the most widely known LGBT babies in the country. One Sunday morning in particular brought this into focus for me. We had just put the girls in their stroller outside the Chelsea Market in Manhattan and I was closing the hatch of our car when I heard, "Is that Juliette and Alyssa?!?!"

I may have looked familiar, and the *And Baby* sticker may have helped those young women put two and two together, but I remember an overwhelming, panicky urge to shield our children from this invasion of our privacy. I had exposed them, and now strangers were recognizing them and felt entitled to ooh and aah over them.

After I had a chance to reflect on this, I ended up adopting a different stance. If I urged others to speak out in *And Baby* despite the impact it could have on their daily lives, I had to embrace that impact myself and to find other ways to keep my family safe. So I instituted a ring of privacy around our increasingly porous lives.

To this day, I, a person who loves open spaces and glass walls, am powerlessly drawn to tall cast iron gates and can't wait for trees to line our driveway and grow to block out the neighbors, despite the fact that I really like them.

———

X and I made an agreement that no matter where I happened to be, I would call home before the kids went to bed. I usually caught them right before or right after their baths and listened to them rattle on about their day—what sissy did, what happened at the park, and endless stories about oh-so-funny Jack.

The babies were now about twenty months old and absolutely hilarious. When asked for her middle name at daycare, Juliette, who doesn't have one, said, "Eh . . . Monkeytoes?" (I called her Monkeytoes because the kid has always been flexible to the point of pliability, turning herself into pretzels and fastening herself to me like a monkey.) Alyssa, meanwhile, was using her superior motor skills to help her sister escape the crib on a regular basis; there was so much to explore.

The anticipation of this evening connection with them would start infiltrating my day around dinner. I would catch myself smiling while I washed dishes because Juliette had explained the night prior how she had been helping mommy do the same. If I was out for business, I would start wrapping it up or scheming how I would excuse myself and step outside for a while. For the last half hour before my call to my daughters, I could hardly concentrate.

And then I would hear their voices, marvel at their daily achievements, and weep on the inside that I again wasn't there to witness them.

Then Alyssa stopped coming to the phone. By the time I got home, I often would not have spoken to her for days.

X shed some insight on the issue for me. "Don't you see a

pattern?" she said. "She thinks that if she has cut you off, shortly after you'll come back. This is her way of bringing you home."

But it was torture. Out of the two weeks that I would be in New York, Alyssa would only speak to me for the first six to seven days. Then would come the words, "No Mama!"

Now I was failing her, too.

Within a few months, X herself stopped talking to me, and I doubt it was for the same reason. I would call, and she would just pass the phone to the children—if she picked up at all. We hadn't been intimate since the children were born; first she hadn't been ready, then I don't know why, but there was no inkling that a change might occur there. My distance from my family, the centerpiece of my arduous efforts, was growing. And relative to other forces against us, the miles had less and less to do with that.

I feared that my wife saw *And Baby* as just work—a mass of daily duties that were a mere means to an end, which was family and home. I worried that she increasingly resented the magazine because it wouldn't stay in a tidy box but rather demanded what she saw as rightfully hers. She had stepped away from it, as she always said she would. So my ongoing commitment could only be interpreted as cold betrayal of her and her dreams. But it felt anything but simple for me. I had to keep reconciling what two different sets of commitments needed to look like while coexisting side by side.

I was living two stark contrasts. I was usually crying on the inside because my life felt lonely, bleak, and compromised. But on the outside, the public was increasingly gushing over me, showering me with accolades for my groundbreaking contributions to the community.

At the depth of my sense of isolation, I was honored with the inaugural Entrepreneur of the Year award in 2005, a humbling and joyous acknowledgment from the national Gay and Lesbian Chamber of Commerce. My brother, who lived in DC and worked for the Pentagon, was going to come to the ceremony with his wife. But then, on the day of the event, I was nearly paralyzed with strep throat. I suggested they stay home, sent my acceptance speech in, and lay in bed, in pain and defeat, while somebody else dedicated the award to the many families behind *And Baby* on my behalf.

Having built on the circulation of *And Baby Magazine*, which had reached one hundred thousand, the *And Baby* radio show was at this point serving about 7 million listeners, and the television series was accessible in thirty five million homes through Comcast, Time Warner, and other cable networks. This was a lot of people, a lot of families—often disenfranchised, nearly always shamed—that continually made the choice to join the conversation I started. To the point that they now owned it, and felt rightly entitled to it. I had asked for their loyalty, and once they had given it, it spurred a relentless sense of obligation inside of me.

———

In California, X grew close with my family and they treated her as their own. At the time, I attributed the change in my mother's view of X to me putting my foot down back in Pennsylvania. However, I now recognize that might have had nothing to do with it: Shortly after they met, X sent my mother a letter that read heartfelt, vulnerable, and inviting. She revealed that she loved my mom dearly, spoke of her gratitude for her new family, and explained the likely role of her own family in her earlier behavior with Mom, as she hadn't grown up talking openly, the way my family always has.

And does my family talk. And dance, and hug, and kiss, and play music. X invited upon herself quite a submersion into the affectionate, loud, and affable obnoxiousness of my Puerto Rican family.

The babies were thriving, lavished with attention and adoration. They proceeded to rename my brother-in-law, who lived across the street and was devoted to the twins with abandonment, and, along with my dear sister (their godmother), became close friends with X. "Abudah," as the girls called him, faxed—from across the street, mind you—a corny drawing of a smiley face topped with a patchy thicket of hair to the children every single day. My mom and dad had already been coined "Ummie" and "Umpa" by one of the forty-six grandchildren that arrived before the twins.

Alyssa's dexterity was astounding. For example, the moment she climbed down from her highchair, she snapped back all of its fasteners in a fury, as if racing against herself. Unbelievable, this kid! And when it came to Juliette's ability to communicate, getting to know her was like a déjà vu for my own childhood. And not just for me.

When the children were about two, we sat down for dinner with my parents one night.

"Time to say grace," my mother said, reaching her hands out in an invitation.

"I can do it! Ummie, listen!" Juliette had everybody's attention. "Bless us, oh Lord, for these thy gifts that we are about to receive!" Gasp for air. "From thy bounty! Through Christ the Lord!" Gasp. "A-amen!"

In addition to the presence of my family in our daily lives, I discovered another small but meaningful silver lining to the calamitous California move: being able to drive more often my 1968 Karmann Ghia convertible—coincidentally, X's favorite car of all time (she even admitted that it had motivated her to date me back in the day). As befitted an original, the car was a prima donna and in New York weather rarely left her temperature-controlled, heated garage. In California, in contrast, I could drive her all the time.

I had not yet adopted the children because X and I thought it would be much easier in California. While second-parent adoption was also legal in New York, it was a much more strenuous process there. In California, it required just our signatures, a negligible fee of some $250, and the judge's endorsement.

During one of my stints at home, I remember X putting the adoption papers in the to-do tray on my desk. I felt exhausted, got busy, thought it was a mere formality I would get to soon enough. She may have reminded me once, but I never acted on the papers—a misstep that would cost me dearly.

———

My second day back was really our first day together. The day I flew in, I would be drained from the grilling pace of the previous two weeks. So, after a few disappointing first days, X fell into the habit of taking the kids out to the park for the day. That allowed me to catch my breath, get some sleep, and gear up to be present by the time they came home.

One morning, upon arrival, I witnessed just how good X was at keeping the family organized. I was coming down the stairs when I saw the kids standing by the door, all dressed, lunch satchels safely in their tiny hands, their little backpacks on. And right there with them was Jackson, sitting in anticipation, her own backpack strapped on.

"Okay, all ready?" X inquired energetically.

"Yes, Mommy!"

"Then we are rolling!" And they were off to daycare, one synchronized, punctual unit.

Upon arrival in California, Jackson quickly learned the kids' schedule. I learned this when I noticed that every afternoon, she got antsy and sat by the door.

"What's up with Jackson?" I asked X one day.

"Oh, it's almost pickup time," she said. "I told Jack this morning that we would walk, so she is just ready."

Ever since we finally "briefed Jackson in" during X's pregnancy, she had seemed to see her responsibility as that of an older sibling. She no longer slept by our bed but rather on the landing, and every night before calling it a day, she checked on the children by looking into their beds. She became their never-tiring playmate and the most dependable babysitter we ever found, attentive to every sorrow, joy, and inconsequential drama.

One day, she even participated in staging a strike.

"No school!" Alyssa announced that morning—concisely, as usual. To X's surprise, nobody was getting ready as per their routine. In fact, the children and Jackson plunked themselves down in front of the TV and refused to get up.

"Well, I am still going to school!" X said, visibly hoping to sway the children. She even went out and got in the car, thinking that at least Jackson would follow—but after driving around the block, she came back to find them still sitting on the couch. Jackson had truly become the best ally the kids could have wished for. I was grateful; they were forming the kind of bond with their dog that had so enriched my own life.

With my kids and Jackson in tow, my old rituals got a few new twists. I tried to surf on at least one of the weekends I was back in California. When I got home, I would throw my board on the lawn to wash it, and before I could return with the hose, Alyssa would have hopped on top, rock-star blond curls flying. I would spray the water over the board, the way the waves would glide over it in the ocean, and she would bend her knees, widen her stance just so, and balance with her arms out, gaze focused on the imaginary beach.

When I took the kids to the beach with me, their favorite game was Sand Monster: after swimming, Jackson would roll in sand so that you couldn't see any black, only her eyes glistening, and the girls would chase her, the sand getting the better of all three of them. It was hilarious!

One of those times when all my girls joined me at the beach I discovered the toddlers' true priorities. Jackson and I ran off into the ocean, leaving X and the girls all settled on the sand. Walking back, I saw that the girls were bawling their little eyes out, distraught beyond belief. I rushed to comfort them that I was okay. X raised her eyes at me knowingly. "It's not you," she said. "They are worried about Jackson."

I looked back over my shoulder; the dog hadn't quite had enough and had stayed back when I got out of the water, surfing the waves and inevitably getting hidden from sight every now and again.

——————

X took the girls for a walk every day after dinner. The nights I joined in the routine often involved two blocks of what I perceived to be reminders of my ineptitude as a parent.

"This is so and so," X would brief me, "they are always here together as a family. And this is such and such, he teaches his kid how to ride a bike every evening."

When I was home, X took Fridays off so she could have some time to herself. On those days I took the kids to my parents' house, where they would spend the day in the pool, soaking in their grandparents' kindness and wisdom. At the end of the day I would bring them home fed, bathed, and ready for bed.

One time, I booked X a surprise stay at the Trident in San Francisco, which had been my mainstay for years the way that Le Montrose had been in LA. I got her a nice room for Thursday night so that she could have some time to walk around San Francisco, visit a museum, and pamper herself. She had stayed there with me before, so I hoped that it would be a relaxing getaway. But she came home early on Friday, in the middle of me and the kids baking, playing, and having all kinds of fun.

"Hi!" I said. "How was it? What did you end up doing?"

"Nothing. I was miserable." She was visibly livid with me. "I didn't leave the hotel."

I had not at all anticipated that answer, and I didn't know what was happening for her—she wouldn't say. I wondered if it could have anything to do with postpartum depression, which she had on several occasions suggested she might have had. But despite my good intentions and regardless of what caused her anger, one thing was clear: I was absolutely to blame for it.

Furthermore, I wondered if the fear I had discovered a couple of years earlier was coming true. It had come out of a dream that turned into a nightmare: X and I were having a conversation, and it was palpable that she hated me because she was a miserable empty nester. "What happened to my life?!" she screamed at me, and I jolted awake, flabbergasted.

At that point, it was only the three of us—her, me, and Jack—and we were only occasionally bumping into the reality of her wanting nothing else, it seemed, from her life besides children.

I woke X.

"One day, our kid is going to go off to college, and what are you going to do? Are you going to look at me and hate me for ruining your life?"

She didn't react strongly, which was not unusual. I will never know whether she thought I was panicking for nothing or stating the obvious, but somehow we went back to sleep, and our shared life continued to track along toward the babies. However, the fear that my wife's whole existence was defined by parenting, that I was peripheral to this singular drive, lodged itself deep inside me. It had remained largely dormant since that dream—but now it was emerging with fresh power.

My next faux pas came from an attempt to give X a bit more of a break when I could. I started taking the girls out to breakfast on Sunday mornings, which also gave me some quality time with them. My first attempt was a false start: we waved Mommy good-bye and piled in the car but didn't manage to get halfway to the restaurant before the girls started whimpering in the backseat. Alyssa got my attention and put both of her chubby arms in the air, which Juliette translated as, "Where is my blanket?" She never left the house without it. I was also adorably criticized for the missing sippy cups. I turned the car around.

When I pulled into the driveway, X was already standing in the doorway, her arm outstretched with the diaper bag. While one might have found this situation humorous, the expression on her face made it clear that she did not. I felt ridiculed; how could I possibly get this wrong, she seemed to be thinking, regardless of the fact that she was getting full-time practice while much of my time went to the not-so-frivolous cause of keeping us afloat as a family?

Once the children attested to having everything they needed for comfort, we were once again on our way to the first of many Sunday breakfasts together.

I wonder if by that time X was already so miserable and uncomfortable in her life that I could do nothing right by her. Shortly after that incident, she said, "I feel like you are outgrowing me." That was one of those few moments I remember her speaking to me from the heart.

———

As always, my publicist had me doing many PR appearances. While I never faltered in my exclusive commitment to X, I would often get hit on at these events. At times, my publicist would have to fend off the attention I wasn't seeking and other times grudgingly accept that I was leaving early to avoid it altogether.

One time was different. Logistics made it easier for a crew-member to stay at the office for a week. It was common for staff and crew to stay over occasionally, so I didn't think twice about it. However, my interactions with other women had been fleeting; in this case I got to know my temporary roommate, albeit purely through the lens of work. One night we were walking to dinner, chatting under a shared umbrella because it was pouring outside, and for a brief moment she put her hand on the small of my back to usher me through the door of the restaurant.

I got shivers all up and down my skin. I didn't act on that

feeling, as I had not acted on any of the other opportunities I had been presented with. But it forced me to face the fact that my marriage was in trouble.

By this point in our relationship, the pang I felt at the obvious lack of intimacy between me and X was second only to my unrequited desire to share *And Baby*'s achievements for our community with my wife. But X had made it clear that her first appearance on that red carpet would be her last, so it was always just me. I had to get used to fielding questions about her with answers that now referenced the many reasons she had to stay home.

———

At some point, "home" came to refer to a new house. We had stayed in the first one, across from my sister, for less than a year when, from out of nowhere, we received a call from the owners.

"Michelle, as you know, the housing market is booming," they said.

Their tone immediately made anxiety bottle up in my throat. "Yeah . . ."

"Well, we have received an offer, a really good offer, to sell the house."

I stayed silent.

"We know that you guys have made it your home. You've been great tenants. And we would love for you to stay. Would you make a counteroffer?"

I could not fathom spending upward of $700,000 on a house in the burbs, nor did we have the money. Abruptly, we were moving out. While we had never seen that house as a permanent solution, the forced move shook our fragile stability.

X found the house she wanted and asked that I call the owner and negotiate. I did, and my family had a new home. I hadn't even seen the place; I was in New York that week.

The time had come for the release of the next tranche of the budget, to initiate the next two dozen episodes of the *Here Family/ And Baby* TV show, but the network had started stalling. I was aware that it was going through a massive upheaval but didn't know whether it would affect me until the payment did not arrive within two weeks of its scheduled date. By the time the network was six weeks late, I knew things weren't looking good at all for us.

For a few months, we couldn't get any communication out of them. I knew this couldn't be good, and it was even worse because I couldn't go elsewhere: I had signed away my right to go to another network. That's the common downside of highly lucrative contracts.

Fortunately, another network that was interested in me tabled a proposition that was not restricted by my contract: they wanted me to executive produce ten different series. In time, when the rights to *And Baby* reverted to me, I would host my show with them as well.

It seemed part of my career's natural trajectory. I loved working with the program director and VP, Carol, at the new network, and the deal—which would have amounted to $4.5 million— would have ensured my family a whole new level of financial comfort, even if I produced only a few of the slated series.

We proceeded in good faith, and I received half of the $50,000 toward producing the pilot of one of the series that I brought to them—*Hammer & Nails: Never Send a Man to Do a Woman's Job*, a show about the fascinating, often humorous lives, work, and personalities of lesbian women in construction.

One time when we shot close to home, X showed up on set with the kids and brought lunch. This felt foreign to me. She had never done this before, and she would never do it again.

We had been barely communicating for about six months.

We tried couples' therapy in California. We got as far as the third session before I walked out. I had been the only one talking; X had met the sound of both my voice and the therapist's with silence. The new house was a telltale sign that I seemed unwilling to heed. I didn't recognize myself, or even my life with the children, in it at all. X had chosen a Cape Cod with a white picket fence around a small but proper and tidy front yard. Too small for us, but just right for a single mother. She had also decorated it into an immaculate mirror of their life together, in which I was a visitor—someone invited to feel at home, but in that way that restricts the guest to carefully designated areas, her behavior governed by an unspoken set of rules. I didn't have the energy to acknowledge this, or to do anything about it. So I just made my time at the house all about the children.

I realized how far gone things were the day we wrapped up the shoot and went out with the crew to celebrate. It had been years since I had laughed, ricocheting joy, basking in achievement and in good company, and letting the music rock me, in that way. *Oh*, I thought, *there I am!*

I could no longer deny that X expected me to change. Hands down, I would have said she actually hated my life. I am not sure, however, whether she had ever considered the practicality of the change she envisioned. My trade was publishing, branding, and marketing; the East Bay was not a hub of the best jobs; and an average job would not have taken care of my family, especially since X was sticking to the non-negotiable condition she had voiced when we got together: that she would stay home once the children were born. Her ambition for simple pleasures in life, lack of pretentiousness, and indifference toward fame were precisely the things that had attracted me to her, and they remained qualities I respected, even if they forced me to adjust my hopes for our life together. What I do not understand to this day is when what *I* represented and strove for became so distasteful to *her*.

One day, one of my closest friends, who had known me since I was in my twenties, said to me, "Mikie, I have known you your whole life. You have always wanted the same things: working in multiple cities, and having more than one home, staff, and a nanny. You have never wavered from that; this is the track you have been on forever. Where the heck did X ever get the idea that you would change?"

Each time I boarded the Sunday-morning flight to New York, I was left alone with the reality that my family was falling apart, and uncontrollable tears would seep through the tension of holding it together. When I finally walked through the heavy door of my Brooklyn loft and put my bag down, I sighed as if I had been holding my breath. I was heartbroken, sick, and defeated. Neither I nor X was living up to our hopes for the other. Our "new normal" was being held together with silence.

CHAPTER 6:
LOSING MY CHILDREN

FRACTURE: the act of breaking; state of being broken.

As I approached the house, my steps were heavy, reticent. The lawn was bare, devoid of the usual signs of my girls' explorations. I reached the threshold. The key hesitated in the lock, but the door opened, callously exposing me to the reality that my family was gone.

The home had been mostly reduced to boxes, encroaching from everywhere. Jackson was aimlessly wandering among these mementos of our loss. Her lower back was barren, and the hair had receded also from her hind legs; her beautiful coat had been devastated by fleas.

I have even let my dog down. She was allergic to fleas, which had not been a problem in New York, but there in California, in the heat, they thrived.

It was July 26, 2006.

I stumbled into the garage and buckled to the floor. Hours passed as I leaned against the walls or lay on the cold concrete, sobbing, wretched, in the ancillary space of my children's world, now disassembled and left behind. The events of the past four months were circling, shrieking, picking at my slain spirit.

———

The bottom had been dropping out of my business, and it was taking my marriage with it. As the income dried up, so did my partner's acceptance of the person she had once claimed to love. I am sure my own stress did not help. I was a jerk to her, strained beyond words, short-tempered, and in freefall, frantically working to keep our life from shattering.

But it cracked in a way I never expected.

It was evening. I had flown in the day before. The kids were sleeping. We were in the kitchen, arguing—which, in our case, meant me talking, trying to reach X, imploring her that we needed to do something about us because things weren't working. She would not engage.

"Come on! Talk to me!"

Silence.

"This isn't working, and you know it! We must do something!"

No response.

"Talk to me, dammit!"

I was stuck in a demoralizing replay of the only conversation we were ever having these days: a one-way dialogue with an absentee party. My voice was escalating, but it felt like she had shut me out and would not let me get through to her. Her silence, her stoic indifference, mocked my efforts on behalf of our marriage.

"I know it has been difficult," I said, trying again. "I know there is never enough money. But what do you think I am doing out there but trying to figure it out, to make money every way I can, to keep us afloat? You know that I am doing everything I can to take care of you and the kids!"

Finally, a response from X. "And you aren't even doing *that* well!"

Slap! Before I could stop myself, my hand flew out and struck her cheek.

She still stood with her back to the stove, frozen.

I still stood in front of her, mute.

Time stopped. The air hung dense, leaving me momentarily breathless before bursting into my lungs with daggers of remorse. I had done a horrible thing. The vacuum expanded between us, edging out any remnants of our relationship. Whatever might have been uttered wasn't heard. I knew in that instant that we would not recover from this.

That night, I slept in the spare bedroom downstairs, the room where I had slept for months, ever since we had moved to the Cape Cod. I felt heavy, ashamed, and disgusted with myself and our situation. The next morning, early, I left the house. It seemed to be the only appropriate action after I had backhanded my wife.

I stayed with my best friend for a couple of days and started looking for a temporary place. I flew back to New York earlier than planned.

———

X and I continued to talk on the phone, exclusively about formalities surrounding my daily catch-ups with the children. And she might have gone on living like that forever, but I couldn't push our issues under the rug anymore. I aimed to raise our daughters with a sense of agency, a trust in their power to create their reality. As long as I had a say, they wouldn't grow up settling, beholden to others, or victimized by circumstances. The very reason I brought them into this world compelled me to demonstrate to my daughters that one didn't have to stay in an unhappy situation—even if it would be years, decades, before they understood. Raising them to become strong women, laying the world at their feet, that made sense. But that's the only aspect of our family that any longer did.

Furthermore, I knew that with X, my family, my colleagues, and my friends alike, I would be the one left to pronounce that the emperor had no clothes, even if it brought relief to all. It seemed to me that everybody always left it to me to say what needed to be said, and I didn't expect that to be any different when it came to our marriage.

———

I was back within the usual two weeks, having braced myself to act. After attending to the kids' needs, we had sequestered ourselves in X's office.

"We need some time apart," I said.

"So you're leaving?"

"Yeah."

X showed no emotion. I could see in her eyes that she was probably hurt by the whole thing, but nothing more was said. She remained behind her desk as I walked out of the room.

It took me but ten minutes to pack up everything I had in the house into my two-seater car. The second move had taken place almost entirely without me, and the rest of my things were in Brooklyn. The broader meaning of me moving out was left open-ended.

It was early March 2006, sunny and in the low fifties as I drove off to an apartment I had rented in Oakland. It was going to give me the space to figure out what to do next—what coparenting needed to look like, and what we both needed, including from each other, to continue our separate lives.

Except that I never got much time to breathe, let alone to reflect, plan, and try to engage X.

Given the good reception garnered by the *Hammer & Nails* cast (which I announced at the Dinah Shore event in Palm Springs, a cornerstone on the lesbian calendar), as well as by some early footage we had sent to the network, we got the green light to move forward and finish the pilot. We were getting ready to draw down the balance of the $50,000 when Carol called me.

"We need to meet." Her usually vibrant voice was distorted by anxiety. "Some shit is going down here with the network."

We met right away. It turned out that the Feds had paid the network a visit and dropped a range of blood-chilling terms, including "misappropriation of funds" and "back taxes owed."

"Michelle, I honestly don't know what's gonna happen here," she confided. "Frankly, I don't even know what I will encounter when I show up for work in the morning."

She was right. Within a week, she couldn't get into the office; it had been locked down, literally. Massive chains constrained the doorway, parading the IRS logo. Not long after, they shut the network down.

Needless to say, my deal was off the table. By that stage, it had been four months since I had received any payment from the network hosting *And Baby*, and the $25,000 from the pilot was barely enough to produce it. The monthly outgoings in California were $5,200, and X continued to expect that sum after I moved out. Everything I could amass went to her and the kids. I would drop the cash directly in the mailbox, always calling ahead to make sure the kids weren't playing in the front yard when I did; my priority was to minimize the disruption to them regarding what was happening, spare them the confusion of seeing me when I wasn't at home with them, and shield them from the tension between their parents. The one time they accidentally saw me on the road, they screamed inconsolably even after both X and I pulled over to comfort them, to lie that I had just arrived and would be seeing them shortly. This experience made it clear to me that hiding the turmoil from them was the right thing to do.

But there was never enough money. I looked for projects with the relentlessness of a tigress. I even took a few custom painting jobs. While I loved to paint and was really good at it, it felt humiliating—a giant step back from where I had gotten to. But my family was in dire need, and painting was my saving grace once again. "Girl, suck it up!" I told myself, slapping my ego in check. "Don't be ridiculous! Be grateful that you have this opportunity to make money. The Universe will provide, but it doesn't always come packaged how we like it."

I called every night to speak to the kids. I felt as if, with every muscle in me, I was pushing against the world to create for my family the space to determine our future.

———

One day, I got a call from X. She was bawling.

"I can't take care of the kids on my own. I can't do this!"

"I can come right now and pick them up for a few hours, if you need a break," I said.

But as soon as I said it, X shifted tacks. The vulnerable tone gave way to anger at me, at how bad a parent I was. Until she hung up the phone.

I called back later that evening.

"Yes?" She sounded annoyed but collected.

"Hey." There was nothing I felt I could do or say to dissipate her antagonism, but I wanted to help and to be there for my girls. "How about I come by tomorrow and take the children for a few hours?"

"Fine." Curt, obliging, baffling to me, she agreed.

I had them all that day, but I took them back to X in the evening. At that time, they never spent the night with me in Oakland.

They were barely three and clung to their routine. It was already strange and unsettling enough for them to have me around but not at the house without bringing them to a strange apartment.

For many couples, this could have been the end of the drama and the dawn of the post-divorce phase of their lives. For X and me, it was only the beginning of our strife.

In mid-July, 2006, X called me while I was in LA, working. The phone rang while I was in a meeting, so I stepped away to get more privacy.

"Hi, everything okay?" I asked.

"The kids and I are fine. I wanted to let you know, though, that I'm going to go spend time with my parents in Florida."

My heart began to pound and I felt nauseated, but I tried not to show my distress. I said simply, "Oh, okay. How long will you stay there?"

"I don't know; I just have to get out of here for now."

I commanded myself to separate what was good for her from how it did not at all feel good for me, since clearly she would be taking the children with her.

"You'll need to take care of the house, and to pick up Jackson," she continued.

"When do you go?"

"Tomorrow."

My heart sank. "Tomorrow?" *And you are only telling me now?* But she needed her family. And the children would have the opportunity to get to know their other set of grandparents. This would be temporary, and I would make myself be okay with it.

"The town car is picking us up and taking us to the airport. I wasn't going to tell you, but your sister insisted that I do it or she would."

My sister and her husband, who had become very close with X and had continued to see the children several times per week even after we moved to the second house, had known about X's imminent trip for weeks and even helped her pack. I respected that my sister had implored X to tell me rather than going behind her back.

"Just please," X said, "don't show up here before then. You can call back later and speak to the children."

I called that night. They were all chatter and excitement. "We are going to go see grandma and grandpa! Mama, we're going to the beach!"

———

The next day, I found myself in an empty house. Yesterday's conversations felt like they had happened a lifetime ago. Now I was on the floor of the abandoned garage, amassing ineffectual resistance to these unsympathetic, fragmented memories, with my children on the other side of the country.

I heard from X within a couple of days.

"I gave notice to the landlords," she told me.

I felt numb, exhausted by my efforts to tune out what my intuition was screaming at me about the gravity of this situation. What my ex-wife *didn't* say was usually what gave me the most insight. It turned out that she had persuaded our landlords to let her break our lease, telling them something about this trip that I didn't know. And she had left me to pick up the pieces, despite the fact that by this point they hated my guts—as did everybody else who perceived me as just another deadbeat spouse who had abandoned her wife and twins.

"What do you want me to do with all the stuff?" I asked, a practical question.

"I don't care." Her voice was indeed indifferent. "You can throw it away."

I didn't do that. I put it all in storage. Which is why I have everything from our life together, from furniture to photos, even my ex-wife's painting supplies and the pack about the kids' donor. There was one item I never found: a family portrait where each one of us occupied a quadrant. It was the only painting X had made during our time together, and she destroyed it with her own hands in the weeks prior to leaving.

I later found out that during this time, X also told a few family members and friends that I was going through a midlife crisis, having an affair, and was back on drugs. It was a perfect myth; from the outside, it would frame me as the source of all our problems and vindicate her every action. There is nothing like a shameful rumor to attract bottom-feeders, revving up a feeding frenzy and satiating their egos at my expense. I believe that energy, disparaging and unjust, was a factor in how drained and betrayed I felt during that time. I have since pruned my world, expunging it of many such vultures.

———

All my houses were gone. I was living in a rental in Oakland, falling apart with nothing but its walls to hold me together, and crying every day. I started counseling, just myself, and cried for three weeks straight; we could never get to discussing anything. Frankly, I was astounded that somebody my size could generate so many tears, but I was a bottomless pit that only got deeper whenever I realized that X had never fought for me. Not once did she let me think that she wanted to save our relationship, find a way to keep us from divorcing. She never showed emotion—not even when I backhanded her, not even when I moved out. It was as if she had been gone long before I walked away, as if I had been the only one still in our marriage.

Nevertheless, I did whatever self-coercing I needed to do in order to support her trip to Florida. I had made a choice to transition our marriage to whatever form it would take while we raised our children. I suspected that it might get worse before it would get better. But nothing could have prepared me for the gravity of what would ensue.

———

Once the initial shock of their departure subsided, our family life kind of resumed its course, the physical distance becoming one of the parameters I was navigating.

My children were now in Florida, which at the time was one of the most homophobic states in the country. I placed a discreet phone call to a trusted contact at the National Center for Lesbian Rights (NCLR).

"We are trying to keep this really under wraps, but you may know that X and I have separated." I spoke more slowly than usual, wading through tears of pain as much as embarrassment and fear. "We have been living apart for a few months." I continued, explaining the facts. "I know I have not followed my own advice. I never adopted the children when I had the chance."

My friend and colleague consoled me, never once passing judgment, never once saying what she could have—namely, "You were the creator and publisher of *And Baby*. For goodness' sake, girl, why in the world didn't you practice what you preached? You knew what was on the line and still made a mistake that you may never undo!"

Instead, she addressed the situation with kindness and quickly moved into action, all the while treating me with dignity and grace.

Meanwhile, X and I were talking every day, like we always had. In fact, we were communicating better, engaging more deeply than ever. I thought that being with her parents was giving her the space to start reimagining how she and I would go on, and I welcomed it.

X shared that she had quit smoking, cold turkey, upon arrival in Florida because she didn't want her parents to know she smoked. I was proud of her. She had also quit just like that when she found out she was pregnant but had taken it up again in the last couple of years. I wouldn't be surprised if our financial and marital stress both served as factors.

One phone conversation of those weeks stood out. I was in LA, driving somewhere, about to get on the 101. X sounded really happy. It got my attention because it had been a while since I had heard that voice: higher tone, more inflection and energy. I thought about it for a few minutes after we hung up, and then I called her back and said, "Hey! You don't have to tell me, but I was just wondering, are you seeing someone?"

After a short, relaxed pause, she answered, "Well, yeah, actually, I am."

I felt happy for her and hopeful for us. I was also dating intermittently. Perhaps this meant we were on a healthy path to crafting separate lives while raising our kids together. Perhaps it meant we would be all right.

She also often had hilarious stories about the children for me. On one of the calls, she said, "Oh my god, guess what: today the kids outed me!"

She was in Florida, at her parents', with our kids. Everybody she ran into of course assumed a husband was lurking somewhere.

"We were hanging out with this new friend I met," X went on. "She was in the passenger seat and our girls were in the back with her kid. Then Alyssa starts talking about Mama! The other kid is like, 'Uh, isn't *this* your mom?' I couldn't believe it."

I could again hear that laughter in her voice that I hadn't heard in such a long time.

I expressed my concern to X that if anything were to happen to her, our children would become orphans because I would not be recognized as their other parent. She agreed, and we enlisted the help of an attorney to develop a parenting plan.

X's undefined visit to her parents stretched into months, and I eventually accepted that my family was living in Florida. Nothing was holding me in the Bay Area, and the children would be much more accessible if I were on the East Coast, so I decided to go home to New York (I still had my space there) and start over. I talked to my landlord, who had witnessed the hell I was living in, and she graciously let me out of the lease.

The next time X and I spoke on the phone, I shared my thinking.

"You are going to New York?" Her voice carried a tone of disapproval.

"Yes. You're not here. You're in Florida. I'll be closer to the kids if I'm in New York."

She dropped the subject.

In order to muster up the cash to start anew, I bought a trashed property that was going into foreclosure with my nephew with the intention of flipping it.

In November, I came to Florida for a few days. The kids were so excited, their rattling didn't stop for hours, not until I was duly filled in on all the happenings. I took them to Disney World, and they had an amazing time. I was soaking up their presence, and X seemed relaxed and comfortable.

It hit me that this was the very first time we had ever been on vacation together. We never went on a honeymoon, and work had played a role every other time, often serving as the reason to be wherever we went, even if we arrived a couple of days before the actual work began.

We all shared my hotel room. X took one bed, and the kids slept with me in the other one. One of those nights, X went on a date—which was still a bit strange for me to stomach—and stayed out until some two o'clock in the morning, when the kids were already sound asleep in my bed.

When it was time to drop me off for my flight, the girls started crying in the backseat before we even approached the airport. Their distress ripped through me. Once we stopped, I got in the backseat with them.

"It's okay, girls! Mama gets on flights a lot, right?" I was smiling, putting on a hell of a show. "I will see you soon, I promise."

It is painful enough to console your children when you are inconsolable yourself, but I also felt dishonest; I had no idea when I would see them. But they calmed down, and I kissed them a thousand times each before getting out and waving goodbye through the passenger door window. When the car pulled away, I dragged myself behind a wide column and crumbled to the pavement. I was choking back tears, my chest heaving uncontrollably. It was a while before I made it into the terminal.

———

Several days later, during one of my regular calls to Florida, X broke down.

"I cannot do this anymore, I cannot stand being here." She sounded distraught, her voice unexpectedly earnest.

"Okay," I said. "What do you want to do?"

"I have to get out of here. I need to come back." She never alluded to getting back together, and I didn't ask about that. I still don't know whether that was her intention. Either way, I wasn't going to exploit a clearly uncomfortable state for her.

"I'll take that house," she said, referring to my property project.

X had told the kids, and their excitement filled my soul. "Mama, we are coming back to California! Be waiting for us!"

She needed me to make this happen, and I sprang into action. I booked their airline tickets. My girls would return right before New Year's, so I had only a month to whip the place into shape—unfortunately, as was habitual for me over the holidays, I came down with bronchial pneumonia and was sick as a dog. But Jackson and I stayed at the property anyway, sleeping on the blow-up bed. A little pneumonia wasn't going to stop me from working around the clock through Christmas, until everything worked properly and I could move our furniture in, stock the kitchen, and make the beds.

I cut a deal that would enable X to buy the house from us, in her own name, without me attached in any way. To make this possible for her, I was going to prepay her a year of child support. To get that money, I sold my sports car and shortly relinquished something much more significant.

And Baby had attracted suitors before, but I wasn't ready to sell. It was my retirement venture, and I did not want to cut me or my family short by selling before its time. And then a suitor presented itself in a way I least expected: I received a call from my trademark attorney.

"Michelle, hi! Look, a company out of Spain is interested in purchasing the *And Baby* trademark."

The offer was negligible.

"You're kidding me, that little? No way!" I took the offer as a slap in the face and sensed something iffy. "Obviously, they either have infringed or are about to infringe on it, otherwise why would they call you and not Chris?"

The intentions behind their move were obscure. The brand was not publicly up for sale. A company looking to do an acquisition would typically have gone through the appropriate channel and contacted my corporate attorneys.

After much negotiation, I settled on a higher offer, though it was still a mere fraction of the exit value I had been positioning for.

Defeated and humiliated, I took the money, and it went toward some of the bills and debts of *And Baby*.

———

"I am not coming."

It was a mere two days before X and the children's scheduled arrival, but now X was telling me this on the phone, resolute and solemn. I knew that voice; she had made up her mind. Later, I learned that her father had talked her out of returning to California and promised to buy her a condo in Florida if she just stayed.

"How could you do this to me? Fucking me over like this?" I was pissed off. I had again dropped everything I had been doing to secure a home for her. I had passed up on a number of potential buyers for the house and was in deep debt. But the stress of all that paled next to what I felt as a stab in the back. I felt like I was being treated like a puppet, like my desire to have my children back was being exploited.

X did not answer me. She did, however, say, "Oh, and don't claim the children on your taxes for last year—my father is."

In light of the bigger blow she had just cast, I didn't have much to say to this one. I felt defeated. I was their other parent and had been working myself into the ground for them, but I felt X was dismissing my ability to provide.

"By the way," she added, "my father said that you should be put in jail for not sending more money."

Clearly, all I was good for in their eyes was financial support.

———

"Mama, Mama! We are not going to California, we are going to Colorado!" I was getting progressively concerned as the kids shared this news with me three nights in a row during our daily calls a few weeks later.

"Hey, Monkey, please put Mommy on the phone."

When X picked up, I snapped, "What's the deal? Why are the children talking about going to Colorado?"

"Oh, it's nothing, I just had to go to Colorado for a couple of days on business and promised the kids I would take them the next time."

I assumed the business was with an old client of ours and didn't give it another thought.

One day in February 2007, I was speaking with Alyssa when she said, "I don't want to live with Grandma and Grandpa!"

"What do you mean, you don't want to live with them? Aren't you having a great time?"

"I just want to live with Savannah!"

That was Alyssa's new friend. I queried her motivation a bit.

"Savannah's got the best toys!" Alyssa finally said.

"Wait a minute, Bean." I was amused by this conversation. "So you want to live with Savannah and don't want to live with Grandma and Grandpa . . . does that mean you don't want to live with Mommy or with me?"

At that moment, the call got dropped. I assumed we got disconnected and called right back, but I only got the voicemail. I kept calling both X and her parents for a half an hour, which stretched into several days, but could not reach them.

I was starting to worry more and more, and that's when I called my attorney, Ann, who had continued—albeit in a strained manner—to draw out of both of us, through individual calls, how we saw our coparenting.

"I cannot reach X or the kids," I told her, and I filled her in on what had happened. "I thought the call got disconnected, but she has not called me back in several days."

"No problem, I will reach out to her," replied Ann.

But she would never hear back, either. X had cut off all communication.

At this point, my attorney advised me to stop transferring

any money to X's account, which I had continued to do whenever I could, so that she could access the money from Florida.

"Michelle," she said, "her silence is making an amicable split less likely. The law will not recognize any support you have extended. You need to stop."

So I did.

I called X and her parents but only got their voicemail. I reached out to others who could know where she might be and anyone else who I thought might be able to tell me where she was, but it was as if she had vanished. My attorney did the same. I even selected a detective to take the search further because we could not find X. I didn't know where my children were. As they say, "The Universe giveth and it taketh away." Disbelief turned to panic; grief dug its claws into my heart, rivaled only by my anger at myself for failing to adopt the girls when I still could have.

And that wasn't the only decision that was indicting me. I had chosen to minimize the disruption of our breakup with my children, to see them less and not insist that they get used to my new apartment. Parenting was about doing the right thing by them regardless of the cost to me, and that was what I had tried to do. I had also chosen to let them go out of state if that supported my ex-wife through the transition. Now that I had lost them, I could see how the decisions I had made to protect my family had locked me out of it while also dissolving what little protection I might have had in the law.

Days turned into weeks, and weeks into nearly three months, and still I couldn't get in touch with my children and didn't know where they were.

When a heterosexual couple splits up—and at least 50 percent of them do—there are laws protecting the children and parents if one parent decides to move to another state. I had no such protection. In the eye of the law, I was a nobody to my children. My ex-wife knew this and was choosing, every day, to keep it that way.

I woke, walked, worked in a grieving stupor. I barely ate, nursed my cups of coffee without tasting them, and sat among my concerned friends without being there. While the world went on, I was floating within it, stuck outside time, longing for a better future while wading through the excruciating present in deprived slow motion. I existed on a kind of life support: my weeping heart continued to beat despite having been broken. I had thought that the pain of a broken heart was but a metaphor until I lived with this—the most intense, relentless ache I had never felt before.

I took up writing letters to the girls during that time, of course without any intention to send them. I needed to be talking to them, telling them how much I loved and missed them, promising them I would find them. And I willed in my heart to reach theirs, the way my mother has always been tuned into me against all reason and despite distance.

February 20, 2007
Well, girls, it's late and Mama should be asleep; it is 1:00 a.m. . . . I just wanted you both to know that I am thinking of you. You both are the greatest joy of my life. I miss you both more than words can ever explain.

February 21, 2007
I don't expect you two to understand, but I must proceed; your other mother will be served tomorrow with papers. Mommy and I have had a very difficult time communicating this last year . . . I am fighting for 50/50 legal custody. My right to see you both. And speak to you every day. You see, I love you both so much; I am fighting hard to be able to keep my relationship with you both. I don't want to take you guys away from Mommy, but I do want to be a part in your upbringing. Mommy and I both together brought you here. I am your other mother and will always be . . .

March 6, 2007
26 days, I call you every day at 4:00 p.m. Your mother is
punishing me. I am doing all that I can within the law
to see you. Please don't ever think that I have abandoned
you, I have not nor would I ever . . .

March 13, 2007
I wish that my words could express how sad my heart is
without you both. I dream about you guys at night and
think of you both all day . . . I will fight for you two
until the day I take my last breath . . .

March 18, 2007
My heart is so broken the tears won't stop . . . I wonder,
do you think about me, how are you feeling inside, I
hope you talk to Mommy about it. I hope she is not
trying to make me out to be some kind of monster . . . or
have you both just forgotten about me.

March 19, 2007
I just received a very disturbing phone call . . . your
mother . . . has moved you both to Colorado. This is my
first knowledge of this . . . I am fighting for you both,
tooth and nail. I will not give up; please know that I
love you with all my heart and I am trying to find you.

The discrimination I was fighting through *And Baby*,
hoping to relegate it to the pages of history, had turned into
a self-fulfilling prophecy. I wanted to exist in the lives of my
children, but I had little more power than a pencil drawing has
against an eraser that's made up its mind.

My attorneys called a meeting.

"We have to file against X," they told me over the phone. "We are very sorry, Michelle, but she is not surfacing and the time is ticking. We only have a few days left. The law gives you six months to lay claim to your children before it concludes that you have abandoned them. Unfortunately in this situation, the clock has been ticking since long before you knew you had a problem."

My six months had started when I last saw the children in Florida.

"You have to get here right now. We need your signature."

The flight from New York to San Francisco felt like an eternity in which I had to face myself at various points in the past six months. Me in disbelief that filing against my ex-wife might be the only way. Me furious about not having adopted the girls. Me—ever convinced that people can step up to do the right thing—hopeful that I might have a message from X upon landing, voiding the reason for this flight entirely.

I landed around 2:00 p.m. that Friday. There was no message from X, but I kept dialing desperately, pleading on her voicemail for her to call me back, even as I ran to my attorneys' office. The cutoff for lodging my suit was 5:00 p.m. that day. The Contra Costa County Courthouse was an hour and a half away, make it more like three hours in Friday's rush hour traffic. We were literally working against the clock.

I rushed into my attorney's office, eyes wide and crazed, and fidgeted as I went up in the elevator. I stopped running only once I entered the conference room where they were waiting for me.

"Have you heard from X?" I asked. "I have not stopped calling her."

We rang her again, on speakerphone, and I begged her, once more, to call me back right away. "She'll call us back," I insisted, "just give her another five minutes. She will call."

My heart was holding on to the vanishing sliver of hope

that we would not have to go down this path. But my stalling, however well intentioned, was quickly becoming a liability in my attorney's commitment to help me.

"If you don't sign these papers right now, you are going to lose your children, do you understand me?" John, the other attorney at Ann's firm, jumped in my face, so charged his head could have snapped. "SIGN THE FUCKING PAPERS! Just SIGN THIS!"

A pen was shoved into my hand. I scratched my signature onto the pages.

"It is done," my voice, barely audible, sounded serrated, like the edge of broken glass. But before these words ever left my lips, the consequences of my action had already been set in motion. My attorney swiftly sealed the papers into a ready envelope and handed the package to the courier I had hardly noticed outside the conference room door. Immediately, he bolted for the elevator.

Wanting to give me space, everybody dissipated. I, however, remained sitting in that conference room, immobilized by the weight of the decision I had just made. With my head in my hands, I sobbed, broken by knowing that indecision, and any other decision I might have made, would have stripped me of my children forever.

The sun was succumbing to the pull of the horizon, lighting up the bay as if to remind me that it would be back in the morning. My soul wept, grieving the dusk of a life that could no longer be—mourning the loss of those parts of me that couldn't fathom that my partner would ever do this.

———

Having filed against X, my attorneys needed to serve her. They attempted to do so multiple times in Florida but could not locate her. They moved to administer something called subsequent service, serving her father on her behalf. To achieve this, they followed her father for some time until he arrived at home. After he went inside, the process server rang the doorbell, and when my father-in-law opened the door, the server threw the paperwork at his feet. Under the rules of subsequent service, X had been served, and given her relationship with her parents, we had every reason to assume she now knew we were looking for her.

And finally, X did the right thing: she reappeared. It was the second to last time that I recognized the person I had married.

It was past midnight when a call from my attorney, Ann, came through. I was driving home in Brooklyn. I pulled over.

"I just found out that X is living in Colorado and that she has sought legal representation in California."

I was a few days from enlisting the detective I had found. If not for this twist of fate, I might never have found my children, who were now settled in Colorado. X must have hoped to start afresh and without a trace of me.

"That attorney X spoke to happens to be a colleague of mind. She advised X, 'You can't just take the children to another state. If you don't call Ms. Darné's attorney, I will.'"

I listened to Ann, but no words came in response. No thoughts came to make sense of what I was hearing—namely, that my ex-wife's silence over the past months was not a result of something tragic happening to her. She was alive and well, which meant that she had cut me off and then picked up and moved our children to another state, just like that, *intentionally*.

"I will be reaching out to X; I have her number," Ann said. "I will call you tomorrow."

———

The next time Ann called me, she said, "I have spoken with X. 'Two things need to happen here,' I told her." Ann's voice was competent, sturdy. "'First up, I need to schedule a teleconference between you and Michelle. And secondly, Michelle needs to see the children.' So, this is how it is going to go down."

I accepted all of Ann's advice and instruction. I was to speak with X via teleconference in a couple of days, at 2:00 p.m. on April 11, 2007.

"Michelle, are you there?"

I had frozen after hearing my attorney announce that both X and I were on the teleconference call with her. I sat down. "Yes."

"Well, now that both of you are on the line, I suggest that Michelle begin."

I was nervous, my heart crowded with a million emotions. "Before we get started, happy birthday!" Her birthday happened to have been just a week earlier. "How are you? How are the children?"

"I am great, the kids are doing great." To me, X's tone seemed anxious and controlled. "We are living in Colorado." She paused. "I moved here because I fell in love."

Not the answer I was prepared for. A mere four months earlier, she had been due to come back to California with the children, and somehow between then and now she had packed up and moved in with somebody? And in a different state, no less?

Still, I had always said to her that love meant my wanting her to be happy, with or without me, so I asked, "Are you happy?"

Her voice seemed to relax. "I am really happy."

"Then I am happy for you. That has always been the most important thing for me."

We spoke for a few more minutes, and X told me more about the children. For the first time in many anguished months, I felt relief.

I flew to Colorado to see the kids less than two weeks after X and I spoke.

While flying from coast to coast, I had often wondered who lived in the middle—in the dirt, as I had thought of it—and, more important, *why*. I had only been to Colorado once: Prior to *And Baby*, I had a publishing client in Boulder. That client had contacted me, looking for an art director, while X and I were separating, and I had recommended X, hands down, as she truly was the best art director I had ever had. That was the client I had mistakenly assumed explained the Colorado references early on.

Denver International Airport was new and vast, scaled to its ambition but oversized, to my mind, for its reality. A whole series of travelators, escalators, and even a train separated me from the outside. I hurriedly picked up my rental car and commenced the hundred-mile drive to my destination. For the most part, the freeway was as straight as an arrow. Four-wheel drives reigned. Apart from some exits, miles of nothing were punctuated by fields. I saw young corn, a few cows, and much evidence of all things horse country. I would not spot signs of high fashion, or of another brown person, for months.

One retail sign assured me I shared some frame of reference with this place.

"Starbucks!" I cried aloud. "Thank god."

I checked into the local Hilton, where I paced, prayed, and talked to my absent children out loud the entire time until X brought them over.

When the moment came, I took the glass capsule elevator to the lobby. I could see the kids watching me descend, jaws dropped. When the doors opened, they ran into my arms.

"Mama, why did you stay away so long this time? Too long!"

Corralling my tears behind strategically worn, extra-dark sunglasses, I was kissing them, their arms and faces crowding out the world.

They told me all about each other, about the flight over the tall mountains, about the parks they went to. I was soaking up every sound, examining every detail that had changed in the over six months since I had seen them.

"There are many things we can do now, Mama!"

"I can put my shirt on all by myself!"

They had turned four.

Their affection and energy turned our hotel room into a whole world of adventure and new discoveries and subtly began the work of thawing my spirit.

Like magnets, the girls stayed attached to me through the night, and I slept upright with a precious child under each arm.

Then, just as I felt my life, eroded by halts and detours, resuming its course, our time was up. The weekend was over.

CHAPTER 7:
THE BLIND SPOT
OF THE LAW

BIAS: a particular tendency, trend, inclination, feeling, or opinion, especially one that is preconceived or unreasoned.

My mother's velvet, jazzy voice filled my consciousness, singing to me across time and space. The song was "O-o-h Child," an old Motown tune by the Five Stairsteps. My mother always evoked its eternal optimism when I was hurt or disheartened. As I was today.

The beat soothed my spirit, bearing tortured witness to the slow-motion collapse of my world. My character had been soiled, my victories defamed, my very existence denied—and for reasons that were so unfathomable that rejecting them, when they reared their ugly heads, seemed less sane than accepting their surreal power.

My mother's singing morphed into another memory. Me,

in fifth grade and deeply troubled, standing in our vast yard, my heavy head drooping. Her kneeling in front of me, my face cupped in her hands, her eyes fixed on mine.

"Whatever they tell you," she said, "all those people who will help themselves to judging you, you are not what they say."

I had not been to school for about five months, complaining of stomach pain every day and putting my poor parents through the agony of countless, and futile, visits to the doctors to diagnose what was wrong with me. Because I continued to stubbornly hide the real reason. But the previous day, a young intern at Kaiser had figured it out, disarming me: the two boys that had been my best friends had turned on me all of a sudden, belittling me and mocking me to other kids.

I could not go back to school and face this betrayal; I didn't even know what I had done, except perhaps showing them up on the soccer field. Having discovered the truth, my mother made a beeline from Kaiser to my school, and by the very next day, everything went back to normal. I suspect that for fear of my mother (I can't blame the principal), I was progressed to the sixth grade, even though I should have been held back. I wonder if that same day, my mother vowed to drum into me the truths she knew I would need as both my backbone and my life raft.

"This is going to be hard." Her truth was looking straight into my eyes. "The road will get bumpy at times, but the way you survive is you bend your knees." In illustration, her lean, elegant form appeared to be surfing on the grass in front of me, probably sanctioning right there and then my ongoing love for the ocean. "But always, promise me, *always* remember who you are, what you are about, and where you come from."

I promised.

———

Once I was back in New York after my trip to Denver, I called X. I have never been one to hold grudges. I always choose to believe that at any point, no matter how nasty one's record, no matter what has been said or done, a person can turn the corner.

I expected to get voicemail, but X actually picked up. Perhaps by accident, perhaps because I had filed against her and attorneys were now monitoring her behavior; I do not know why, but she did. I pulled over on Twenty-second Street in Manhattan; I remember the call like it was yesterday.

"Hi!" I opened up. "Listen . . . the next time I come to town, why don't we get together? I'd like to take you guys out to dinner, meet Norma." Norma was the woman X was with now. I didn't like that X had moved our children into her house within months of meeting her online, but regardless of how I felt about that parenting decision, it had been made, and I was willing to move forward. "We can spend some time together, talk about the children, about parenting."

X didn't respond; instead, she diverted our conversation to another topic. I tried to reach out a few more times in the following weeks, tagging the invitation onto my calls to the children.

"We should make some time; perhaps a coffee?" I said during one call. "We should probably get together and talk about coparenting."

But while my requests were not rejected, they were not acknowledged, either.

My birthday came in early June. I called the kids at the scheduled time from New York.

"Mama, where are you?" they asked. Childhood curiosity was on the line. "What is that noise?"

I explained to the girls that what they were hearing was the birthday bash my friends had thrown for me.

Allegedly, they got off the phone and demanded that X take them to the airport. She called me, disgruntled, half an hour later and said, "Thanks for telling the kids about your party. Now they won't talk to me, and they are demanding that I put them on the plane so that they can be at your birthday."

I was touched, but that feeling quickly yielded to sorrow. For an absurd reason outside my control, it couldn't be more than this—more than a momentous yearning of our hearts. My ex-wife had instituted invisible boundaries that separated me from my children, prevented me from actually having them in my day, no matter our will or willingness to see each other.

What followed was weeks that morphed into months of waiting for the trial. Filing against X instigated a flurry of hearings, case management meetings, and status updates. The actual trial was set months out, for November 26, 2007.

Family court process is designed with the hope that the families resolve issues on their own. The court's object is the children, and it is deemed best for the children that their parents transition to co-parenting amicably. The Courts take an assertive stance only if there is immediate danger to the children—for example, domestic violence or abuse. Otherwise, the system is designed to minimize the role of a judge in negotiating one's life.

I also learned that when you're in litigation, you spend your life in court. They have you come in for preliminary hearings, for case management meetings, for mediation, for this and for that, until you're a regular, through and through. They give you ample opportunities to pick a favorite parking space; to identify which vending machine doesn't malfunction; to locate the water fountain with the perfect water pressure; to run into other families more than once and conclude that you don't have it so bad; to notice guilt growing inside you that you need to be in family court rather than with your family, whatever its form; and to muster up the courage to have a conversation with your ex-partner and find, however tough, an amicable solution. Finally, you also have plenty of chances to apologetically remove your case, negating the need for a trial and freeing up the calendar for somebody who really needs it.

On all those occasions, the courtroom was usually full, everybody scheduled for that day waiting their turn. I heard some horrific things—horrendous abuse endured by children, by spouses. I remember thinking to myself, *We don't need to be here, taking up this court's time. The judge should be focusing on those cases. Why is my ex-wife taking this position?*

The town where my children were living became synonymous with apprehensive, wasted waiting. There were only two direct flights to New York from Denver on Sundays, so Colorado held me captive through Monday, long after the girls left.

Absent any formal parenting agreement, my attorney monitored a good-will arrangement for me to see my children once a month. It cost me a small fortune—an average of $1,200 per trip for the flights, rental car, hotel room, and meals out—and turned out to be but nothing more than a gamble. Too often, for too many an obtuse reason, I would go back to New York without having even seen my children while in Colorado.

One occasion stands out in particular. There was a torrential downpour in New York that made it all over the news. I could not get on my flight to Denver and had to be rerouted through Los Angeles, where I incurred more delays and an extra $900 in last-minute attempts to get to Denver. During all this I called my attorney, who notified X about the situation.

When I finally got to the hotel early the following morning, I was nearly twenty-four hours late getting into town. Not having slept in two days, I waited. And waited. X was supposed to bring the children to the hotel, but she didn't.

It wasn't until mid-morning that X finally called me, and all she said was, "Well, they are napping now."

My time was scheduled to run out that afternoon. By the time X brought them over, I only had a couple of hours left. And the time I had lost was gone forever; X dismissed any mention of rescheduling due to extraneous circumstances.

Whenever I wasn't flying to Colorado or to California (where I was spending an exorbitant amount of time at my parents' place to accommodate all the court appearances), I was living in New York, in my space in Red Hook, trying to make the money I needed to afford it all.

That was far from easy. I was turning down more projects than I was taking. God knows I needed the money, but I had to walk away from work time and again because most projects could not comprehend, let alone accommodate, my fickle unavailability. I had to refuse a project in Paris that would have yielded $175,000 and say no to my attorney when she offered to pimp me out to a publishing house for an impressive $550,000 per year. I was left mainly with random, second-rate gigs that I held on to, and over-serviced, because I needed the money for court.

Meanwhile, my attorney's discovery file was bulging at an increasing rate as X filed her case paperwork. She had amassed evidence that I was extraneous to our girls' lives; a substandard human being; an absentee ex-partner; and a dubious business-person. These were her children, and I could not possibly qualify to be their parent. Especially since I had to literally overwrite the norms to even suggest my existence: every single form I had to fill out started with the blank for "Father's Name." I did a lot of crossing out and reframing.

The malice X peddled was facts enough for most. Despite legal documents to the contrary, she argued that I had constructed the myth of *And Baby*'s loss of funding to cover up my profound leadership failure. My financial statements, showing the sporadic and insufficient funds, were paraded as proof of my inadequacy.

At some point, this led to a fight between us.

"I tried everything," I shouted in response to her profound disappointment in me. "And you know it! I did anything and everything that I could to make you happy. When I couldn't be there after the children came, I made sure that somebody was, to help you!"

"If you are referring to the help you hired," she said, "then how dare you? I never wanted somebody else raising my kids. And on top of that, you go and hire me a non-English-speaking nanny that I can't even communicate with?"

That is how I found out that she had always resented me even for decisions that I thought I had surely made in order to do right by her.

I also came to learn that many other concerned observers had formed strong views about my parenting and submitted scathing letters on the matter to our swelling discovery file. There were letters praising X as a mother, as well as ample ones condemning me as a parent. One of those came from Josh. My Josh. Single, childless thirty-something Josh, whom I had invited out of waiting tables and treated as a son, accepting every quirky part of his persona, regardless of its fit for the job. The Josh I had effectively elevated into the power of an associate publisher, and to whom I had bared my every weakness for the sake of *And Baby*, so that he could more readily compensate for them.

"She will choose work over everything," was his verdict.

———

One day, Ann invited her partner at the firm to join us in the boardroom for a meeting.

"Michelle," she said, "this is John; I believe you have met." We had indeed met, briefly. "I hope you are okay with this; we've made a decision that John will represent you rather than me. The judge assigned to your case is very tough. John is an experienced litigator, and we believe that his skill set is what we need."

I wasn't sure. I didn't know John, not the way I knew and trusted Ann. And her approach was much more intuitive to me: she negotiated, she believed in the best in people; she strove to uncover, to bring into clarity for each divorced couple an amicable arrangement that they could live with. She believed in win-win solutions, in mitigating compromises; she stood for common sense, for decency. The word "litigator" itself sounded harsh, foreign, and unnecessary. But they had made the decision, and I had only so much fight in me.

———

For months, I lived in a constant state of betrayal as X played the court system to methodically disown my role in the lives of our children, and under the lead weight of possibility of losing them forever.

Ironically, in the hands of this lesbian mother, the "straight" card was used again and again. X presented a position where parentage was her sovereign and exclusive right; I was someone who had to earn it, a task at which I had obviously failed.

I recalled X's comment when a couple of our (lesbian) friends were dealing with significant marital problems. "After what Tammy has done," she said, "Linda will never let her adopt the children." Linda was the biological mom.

Back then, I had dismissed what felt incongruent—one parent's rights being contingent upon the other parent's satisfaction with her as a spouse—but now I was on the receiving end of the position my ex-wife had so casually detailed that day.

Societies create laws for a reason. Laws do not seek to judge people, but they do judge certain actions, with the intention of preventing them. They acknowledge that we aren't always the best people we can be. Often, they are meant to protect us from ourselves—from harm we can cause ourselves in times of intoxication, grief, or other weakness. We generally feel safe getting into our cars because we know that the law has done everything possible—from the harsh consequences of a DUI to traffic lights, speed-limit signs, and the cops that enforce them—to protect us from harm.

If we regulate who is allowed to drive a car, and how they do it, then surely we can deploy the legal system to protect our children from the choices we've made while mourning the end of our marital dreams.

Relationships often end, and too few of us are at our best when we feel abandoned, hurt, or wronged. People do crazy things in the throes of a breakup. Unfortunately, the current models of divorce and family law mean that our children are typically—even if sneakily—put in the category of marital assets and leveraged for financial agreements.

In my story, it does not matter if one of us was more right or wrong when it came to our relationship. This had little to do with either one of us being fit to parent our children. But because of the way the laws in this country were written, let alone where they were missing altogether, one of us had the absolute power to lock the other one out of the right to parent our children. We do not have to accept this as inevitable any more than we have to accept hit-and-runs.

Even more frustrating was that X seemed to expect credit for engaging with me at all on this matter. One day on the phone, she said, "You should be grateful that I didn't stay underground. Everybody told me I should just wait it out. 'Let her keep looking for you,' they told me. 'Very soon, her time will be up, and you will never have to worry about her again.'"

If I had accepted the dire injustice of what was happening, I suppose I would have been grateful. The actions of my ex-wife have only one explanation: she was seeking to exterminate me from my daughters' lives.

During one of our prep sessions, Ann looked me in the eye. "You know," she said, her voice ever compassionate, "one of my associates walked into my office the other evening. The practice had already gone quiet for the day, but she was working on your case. She looked at me in shock, tears in her eyes, and asked, 'How can this be happening to her?' I am, we are all, so very sorry,

Michelle." She took a breath. "Unfortunately, what I believe X is doing is called 'parental alienation.' It is a controversial area of family law in part because it is very difficult to prove; this is a nascent area of psychiatric and legal study. But I do believe that X has been systematically removing you, both physically and emotionally, from the lives of your children."

No kiddin'. . . thank god . . . of course . . . no shit!?! I couldn't believe there was a term and a whole field of study on this behavior.

"John and I will be arguing this in court," Ann concluded.

It wouldn't be until 2013 that *Parental Alienation: The Handbook for Mental Health and Legal Professionals* came out, seeding more books and marking the maturing of recognition of parental alienation as "a parent's purposeful campaign of vilification, characterized by anger, resistant and inconsistent compliance with court orders, conscious or unconscious denigration of the child's other parent, and interference with the other parent/ child relationship."[1]

Parental alienation leads to a "serious mental condition that affects hundreds of thousands of children and families in the United States . . . in which a child—usually one whose parents are engaged in a high-conflict separation or divorce—allies himself or herself strongly with an alienating parent and rejects a relationship with the 'target' parent without legitimate justification."[2] In fact, an estimated 22 million people currently suffer from parental alienation, and it is being increasingly framed and acknowledged as a form of domestic violence.

Regardless of how she may have felt about me as a partner, I never imagined that my ex-wife would stand between me and our children and force me to prove that I had always been their parent. Never did I believe that she would hurt me right where it hurt the most—that she had it in her to attack where I was defenseless.

I had no legal documents to prove that the children were

1. Douglas Darnall, *Beyond Divorce Casualties: Reunifying the Alienated Family.* 2010.

2. D. Lorandos, W. Bernet & S. R. Sauber, *Parental Alienation.* Charles C Thomas. 2013.

as much mine as they were hers. And that was an issue primarily because we weren't heterosexual.

It is a sobering statistic that in some demographics, more than 50 percent of all sanctioned heterosexual marriages, most involving children, lead to divorce. Second marriages have an almost 75 percent dissolution rate. But in a heterosexual relationship, should it end, there is a presumption of parenthood even if the child is conceived outside of the marriage. In a same-sex marriage, in contrast (even if it had been legal in New York), there was no presumption of parentage. Since I hadn't executed second-parent adoption, I was being left out in the cold, even though I was listed on their birth certificates—hell, even though they had my last name. As if any of these details make a parent.

I could still see those adoption papers in my tray before they disappeared under the weight of other documents. What had seemed a mere formality next to the aggressive burden of other responsibilities I faced at the time had now become something that would forever haunt me. The one signature I should have never needed was the one with power to wage a bitter vendetta.

If legal heterosexual marriages at least protect the children from the effect of their parents' emotions, where does this leave the non-sanctioned—and in many states at that time, illegal— alternative families that happen to be raising more than 9 million American children today?[3]

Gay civil rights have long been a hot political topic. Since the Stonewall riots on June 28, 1969, great advances have taken place across the US for LGBT citizens. Slowly, laws are catching up to the changes that have occurred in everyday life. In June 2015, the Supreme Court ruled that states cannot oppose same-sex marriage, effectively legalizing it across the country. Two years earlier, in June 2013, in a widely watched and narrowly cast 5–4 vote, the Supreme Court struck down Section

---

3. A conservative estimate, as it is based on the 1995 National Health and Social Life Survey by E.O. Lauman, which provides this data, currently cited by most credible sources.

3 of the Defense of Marriage Act (DOMA) as unconstitutional under the due process clause of the Fifth Amendment of the Constitution, which prohibits arbitrary denial of life, liberty, or property. DOMA, passed in 1996 by a veto-proof majority in Congress and signed into law by President Bill Clinton, defined marriage as only between one man and one woman.

By declaring that "spouse" does not have to be a person of the opposite sex, these milestones have opened the LGBT community to receiving federal benefits previously granted exclusively to heterosexual married couples.

What benefits? While there are some 1,049 benefits and privileges contingent upon marital status, the widest reaching include insurance for government employees, social security survivors' benefits, immigration privileges, and tax benefits. The lack of equitable tax relief has been especially significant. The landmark case that found its way to the Supreme Court, *United States v. Windsor* (2010), denied a woman a tax exemption of $363,053 when her spouse (to whom she was legally married) died and left her the estate. In compliance with DOMA, the Internal Revenue Service denied the exemption because "spouse" was not applicable to a woman married to another woman. As a result, Edith Windsor sued the United States government and won.

In many US states, LGBT adoption is still illegal, and even where it is not, second-parent adoption may be. Societal assumptions about parenting have not kept pace with the reality of today's diverse family compositions. And the truth is that, in addition to the broad uncertainty associated with the new US administration, a gaping legal void remains around parenting despite the Supreme Court ruling on gay marriage in the summer of 2015.

In my situation, I felt like my ex-wife wanted me to disappear altogether, freeing her to raise our children with her new partner, who could adopt them.

After the demise of any marriage, it is not unusual for the partners to wish the other person could be out of their life forever. A clean breakup, where two people can part ways amicably and move on, is rare. When there are children involved, the primal instincts of love and protection tend to be negatively tweaked by someone who is no longer a lover and is typically not a friend. Add to that hostility and feelings of blame and resentment, and divorce can feel like a prison sentence.

In the case of same-sex parenting in those states where the relationships were not legal, Section 2 of DOMA ensured that the dissolution did not have the legal protection afforded hetero-sexual marriages. Presented with the expected resentments and hostilities, the parent on the outside of the limited structure had to fight harder for the basic rights that would not be in question for any legal heterosexual marriage.

It was strictly because of my sexual orientation that I was presumed *not* to have rights to our children.

It wasn't that X was any less gay than I was. It was that she had physically given birth to the children that we had mutually planned and conceived. The problem lay with whom I had chosen to love, the ineptitude of our legal system, and the prejudice of the people who were interpreting the law.

As the biological mother, X was waived any accountability and was under no obligation to prove that she was a fit mother. Her intentions were never questioned. She was granted an untouchable indemnity; the assumption was that she was always acting in the best interest of our children.

Living in a state with marriage equality offers same-sex couples more protections than they would find elsewhere, but it is not nirvana. Complications still arise because laws have not caught up to societal changes and therefore have not determined how to equitably handle the potential dissolution of these marriages.

No matter the issues between her parents, a loving bond between a child and her non-biological mother does not dissolve in divorce simply because the biological mom no longer finds it convenient to keep her ex-partner in her life. No person should be systematically deleted from the lives of his or her children solely becausehe or she is not the right gender, age, or womb.

———————

It was September 18, 2007, about nine weeks before the trial, while our preparations were in full swing, when a curveball came in via fax.

X had filed for change of jurisdiction from California to Colorado, where she claimed residency. Her argument concluded that "it [was] in the children's best interest [that] any further matters be addressed in our home state of Colorado. As I am their only legal parent, my availability to them must be maintained. My travel back & forth to CA puts their well-being at risk."

John called me as soon as he received my fax. He sounded alarmed as he said, "You cannot let this happen. If you let her win this one, you will most likely lose and never know your children. In Colorado, she's got a partner, a house, some clients—we must not let her bring this onto her territory."

Besides all that, Colorado was much more conservative and overwhelmingly white.

It was too much for me to get my head around. I crumpled to the floor of my loft in New York, only a short distance from the edge. My chest was heaving with devastation.

Jackson, always by my side, dove in to comfort me, acting as the well-practiced life raft she had become.

Cradling my knees in a dire attempt to stay in one piece, I called my mother.

"Mom, this is so hard," I told her. "I don't know if I can do this."

In the months leading up to this moment, I had heard about, seen, and read unimaginable cruelty, including debilitating slander to my character and denouncing of me as a parent.

My account was overdrawn. I had thousands of dollars' worth of outstanding legal bills. Too often, I felt like I could do nothing right by the kids.

"I don't know if I can keep going," I said.

"If you give up on your kids, I will never speak to you again, you hear me?" My mother's tough love was bruising me from the inside out. But it was also talking directly to the part in me that could not be defeated. "I raised you to be stronger than that! Get your ass of the floor!"

I did. And then I called Ann.

"Look, we'll figure out the money thing," she said once I bared to her my less-than-battle-ready state of affairs. "If you are willing to keep going, we are there with you."

My attorneys' stance was one of firm counterattack, and luckily, that fighting spirit transferred to me. Until the petition for change of venue was resolved, the petition to affirm my parental rights could not be heard.

There was no way of knowing exactly when X had filed her petition, but it was clear that we were way behind already. The hearing on the jurisdiction was set for 8:30 a.m. on October 5, 2007—only two weeks away and a mere six weeks before my trial, the endeavor that still demanded every ounce of preparation we could amass.

For now, I had to demonstrate that X had not intended to permanently move away. Those JetBlue airline tickets from Florida to California that I had bought for her and the children were my saving grace. One-way and dated a mere couple of months prior to her disappearance, they were evidence.

The morning of the jurisdiction hearing, X appeared in California court. She didn't look at me. Her body, harmonized to her voice, was foreign, calculated, and heartless. I could not recognize the woman I had met at Ruby Fruits, who had basked in Pennsylvania with me, whose hand I had held on the roof as the World Trade Center came down, who had witnessed the vision of *And Baby* bloom, and who had used the power of her artistic talent to right the wrongs of social injustice. Just a few yards away stood a merciless executioner—a self-made enemy.

The testimony of those involved in the arrangement of X purchasing the house, namely that of my nephew and that of the real estate agent, strengthened my argument that she had intended to return to the Bay Area. California was deemed to be her home state.

"The evidence to move venue for this case is deemed insufficient. The case will remain in California," Judge Baskins declared, exuding the authority befitting his position. X was to be extradited back.

"Your Honor, with all due respect, I cannot afford to travel back and forth," X claimed, "and being absent from my children puts their well-being at risk."

"I'll make you a deal: you don't have to come in; you will do a court call." The moment Judge Baskins finished his sentence, it was clear that he had closed that matter definitively. "Next, this court will consider the matter of Ms. Darné's parentage of two minors. The trial is confirmed for November 26, 2007."

While exiting the courtroom, my path crossed that of my ex-wife, and I took that opportunity to look her in the eye and say, "You just made a wrong fuckin' move! Mark my words: I am not going away."

I felt somebody grip my arm, gently but decisively. "I will fight you to my death for them, and you know it," I continued while my attorney, who had swiftly appeared and took hold of me, led me outside.

When Trial Day—November 26, 2007—came, I couldn't tell if I had slept at all by the time my alarm went off. The skies hadn't yet woken as I lay pensively on my parents' pullout couch, my soul restless and heavy, my thoughts erratic and viscous. Over the last eight months, I had grown used to this state of uncomfortable disorientation, which had plagued me since I stepped into this most important fight of my life. I had considered, ad nauseam, the implications of losing today, and by now—survival instinct, I suppose—I was desensitized to the possibility.

In a few minutes, my mother and father would emerge out of their rooms to make coffee. We would collect ourselves—collect me. I had not communicated with anybody in days. My soul had erected an impassable barrier around its fragile hope, a mile-high wall to shield its inscrutable pain, and that barrier shut out the world and everything that came with it—its opinions, its condolences, its unsolicited advice (quick to project what other parents, with innumerable definitions of the job, would do in my place), its warm embraces, and its awkward silences. For once, the inconsequential sounds of my parents' heater, of the wind that was frazzling the tree outside, and of the rustling of my sheets were getting my undivided attention. Outside of those sounds, the world had become muted. I was inhabiting a silent movie. In its vacuum, my universe had become more insurgent. I was existing in an echo chamber where doubts, regret, anger, pleading, and disbelief resounded back at me with brutality.

In a weird twist of fate, I had lost my phone the night before, which meant I was severed from those close friends who had retained access to me. Thankfully, my wise parents needed no words in order to care for me. And there wasn't much to say, anyway. I had forbidden anybody to go to court with me, including my mother. Today, I could not bear to witness her break if I lost.

———

The court parking lot was thick with the gravity of the day. Despite it being a cool autumn morning, I struggled through every step as if I were walking through hot tar.

The courtroom was vast and consequential. X was to my left, blocked from my view by my attorney and further removed by the space between our two six-foot-long tables. The bystanders, and all those passively observing our case as a necessary burden of getting to theirs, occupied the rows of pews behind us. Ahead and slightly above us was the bench of Judge Baskins— the bench from which he had pronounced truth and resolution for countless families for twenty years.

Crouching next to the judge, apprehensively vacant and confronting me with the treacherous and irrevocable vulnerability to which it was ready to subject me, was the witness stand. The stenographers, sprinkling us with the hurried rhythm of their instruments, were on one side, the bailiff on the other.

"All rise!" the bailiff commanded.

Everyone stood.

"This court is in session. Judge Baskins presiding."

It had begun.

The judge wore his absolute power regally. X, who was representing herself, began presenting her evidence against me. Although her voice, now foreign and calculated, had condemned me at every step in the court process thus far over the phone, this time it was reverberating within mere feet of me, her stare threatening to topple me off the stand.

"Ms. Darné's financial standing is not material to the issue at hand. Evidence dismissed."

"Various opinions on Ms. Darné's aptitude as a parent are not material to the issue at hand. Evidence dismissed."

Judge Baskins did admit into evidence the countless photos of me with the children, dating back to the day they were born. He also accepted the media mentions of us as a family, including our stated intention to have children, references to the pregnancy, and the *And Baby* press release announcing the birth of our girls.

My attorney began his questioning after X took the vow on the stand. "Ms. X, please describe the day you became pregnant."

"It was a while ago," she said. "I do not remember much."

"Was Ms. Darné there with you?"

Silence.

"Did Ms. Darné inseminate you?"

"I do not recall."

I hadn't thought my heart could sink deeper, but at that answer, it plummeted to places I did not want to follow. I felt myself deleted out of the life I had built in plain sight of the American LGBT community. I had been the cornerstone for alternative parenting, and now I exemplified the omissions within an outdated system. I had been the spokesperson of my community, and now I found myself among the millions silenced by their absence in the law.

When all we had both prepared and presented had been aired, a heavy pause encased the courtroom. The room's silence was resonating within mine. I heard hasty scribbling on a note-pad. A few impatient sighs. Somebody coughing. Every minuscule detail of humanity's physical functioning was given stage, reducing all of us to bundles of nerve endings, hardwired for self-preservation and defenseless against instincts.

"This court will now rule on the case of Ms. Darné versus Ms. X."

My attorney's leg was visibly shaking—rhythmic, apprehensive, unnerving. I was barely breathing. My past, my future, my very identity hung in the balance.

"Ms. Darné is affirmed as the presumptive parent of the minor children in question." Judge Baskins proceeded to spell out my rights to time with them, my financial support obligations, and my entitlement to parenting my children to the best of my ability and through all the opportunities I had to offer.

"Don't I get to think about it?" X exclaimed.

"No, I did the thinking for you. It is decided." Judge Baskins paused to let the significance of his statement sink in. "Ms. X, what are you worried about? That Ms. Darné steals the children?"

I am not sure he was aware of the historic irony in his question. "Don't you think that if she were going to do it, she would have done it already? It is good for the children that Ms. Darné travels; they are fortunate to have the opportunities this presents to them. But I will make you a deal, Ms. X. They can't travel with Ms. Darné until they are five. Are you okay with that, Ms. Darné?"

"Yes," I replied.

Despite us never having been legally married, and despite the lack of a formalized second-parent adoption, the judge upheld my parentage. This set legal precedent and became a major step toward equalizing the rights of all citizens to their children. For me, leaving this legacy further vindicated the suffering that birthed it. I won my case because I could prove my role in the children's lives (it helped that ours was a very public family) and because I had the drive, resilience, and resources to do so. Given the torment I had endured, I can only imagine the despair that has been felt by many in my situation who are without those advantages.

Once the court was adjourned, I rose and remained cemented in place, as if frozen by the gravity of what had occurred. My attorney, who was visibly animated by the outcome, stood, strong and unwavering, by my side. The tears of joy that were fogging my vision also glistened, victorious, in his eyes.

Before I realized it, X had crossed the space between us and was pulling me into her. "I am so glad you won!" Her clear hazel eyes meant it, gleaming straight at me with a deep joy as she hugged me. "The children will be so happy! You have no idea the stress I have been under with my parents, with Norma."

As if catching herself, her hands on my shoulders, she pushed me away and repossessed the hostile stance I had grown used to. Her words sounded a stark contrast to her body language as she pronounced, "Now you get to meet Norma!"

My consciousness was still lingering in the moments preceding her embrace; it took a moment for it to catch up with this combustive metamorphosis. Since X's emergence from hiding after those months we had looked far and wide for her, this was only the second time I had seen the woman I had married. It was as if her true self wasn't the one persecuting me but rather the one in the pews behind me, quietly cheering for justice for me and our children.

I did not react to her before I was momentarily moved out of the court so the next baffling family could step into position.

I floated out of the courtroom on the energy of my attorney. My every step felt a bit lighter, more cognizant than the last of the momentous day they were marking.

I do not remember driving back to my parents' house, but my mother was waiting for me. I collapsed into her arms and to the floor the moment I walked through the door, and I proceeded to cry for about three hours. As she held me, she could only conclude that I had lost.

That day, victory felt like crossing, dehydrated and dazed, the finish line of the most draining marathon I never knew I would be running and scarcely hoped to complete. I only had energy for one phone call, to a close friend in New York. Like many of my other close friends, she hadn't slept the night before and had been anxiously waiting to hear the outcome. She called everyone else on my behalf to deliver the good news—thus activating a flurry of calls to my parents' phone.

My mother did most of the updating while I just sat there, drenched in what had happened. Despite having planned, birthed, loved, lost, and found my children, in the eyes of the law I had only just become a mother.

CHAPTER 8:

BLACKHEART

SACRIFICE: the surrender or destruction of something prized or desirable for the sake of something considered as having a higher or more pressing claim.

Barely a week into the new year, I was back in court again, this time for a mediation session that was intended to result in an interim parenting agreement between me and X.

The mediator appeared as I sat in the waiting area of the Contra Costa courthouse. "Michelle Darné?"

"Here," I replied. I stood up and followed her into her office.

"Neither party should communicate with the mediator without the other party present," stated the top line in the *Important Information* leaflet I had received, so I didn't say a word. I just sat there across from the mediator, who in turn sat silent at her desk. There was another chair, empty, next to me. A few feet away, there was a small, inviting round table for those divorcées who got to work things out face-to-face. Although the room felt neither welcoming nor sinister, I was so wired and stressed out by not knowing what to expect that I couldn't get comfortable.

Then the phone rang; it was X calling in.

"Good morning, ladies," our mediator said. "This is the mediation session stipulated by the judge. Today, you will make several very important decisions that will guide how you coparent your children until you develop a permanent parenting plan."

What ensued were a couple of hours in which we got nowhere. Whatever the mediator proposed was met with something like, "I don't want to do that," from X. All we had to go on was her voice, and the sound of it was as defiant as its absence. Several times, the mediator queried, "Ms. X, are you there?"

One topic, however, did get her talking: me looking for a house in town.

"I don't understand why she needs to live here!" X exclaimed.

"Wait a minute, Ms. X," the mediator said. "It is good for the children to have two homes. It is not good for them to always meet at the hotel. Ms. Darné is doing the right thing by creating such an environment for them."

That silenced X—for nearly another hour of unanswered questions and suggestions.

"Ms. X, are you still with us?" the mediator asked again. I could see her temper growing shorter. I did not get a sense that our session had a time limit, but she seemed frustrated that it was sure to last way longer than necessary. "Ms. X, are you planning to participate in this conference call? We have to make some decisions here, which I will need to put in the report for the judge."

I don't know whether X actually felt bad for wasting our time or simply opted to cooperate to preserve a "good girl" façade, but we did move forward in the hour that followed. Even if only an inch.

"I take the kids to church on Sunday mornings, so I need to have them back by 8:00 a.m.," she said.

"Fine," I said.

"Okay, we have made some progress, and we are getting to the end of our time," the moderator said. "This is probably as much as you guys were going to agree to." She seemed resigned to, more than content with, our progress. "You have agreed that neither parent will make, or allow others to make, disparaging comments about the other parent within hearing of the children." I had pushed for that.

"You have also agreed that Michelle will provide the children's physical care the third weekend of each month, from Friday, 8:30 a.m., to Sunday, 8:30 a.m."

Forty-eight hours per month. The extent of my life with my children. But at least I had just been acknowledged as their other mother.

While X had shown herself as alienating, vengeful, and irrational, somehow the system appraised this time allowance as fair. Furthermore, it must have been deemed an acceptable measure of progress, since the mediator proceeded to conclude the session, which had lasted nearly three and a half hours by that stage.

The temporary parenting agreement that came out of that session was enacted on January 16, 2008.

Within a few days, my mother joined me for my next parenting time in Colorado. It was her first trip there, and I gladly welcomed the company. This time, to claim a bit of my own space in a circumstance thrust upon me, I arranged for us to stay at a bed-and-breakfast a bit out of town, on the lake. It was cold and sunny and clad in ample fresh snow.

"You could have told me your mother was coming," X hissed at me when she dropped the children off.

Why? Because you are scared of her and would have liked to put on a good show rather than act the way you always do? But I was no longer married to her and didn't owe her any explanation, so I said nothing.

The girls, however, were ecstatic, and my mom was all joy when they arrived. She had not seen them since they left California a year and a half earlier.

Throughout the weekend, my mother and I kept our eye out for a place for me to rent; we looked at some serviced accommodation and at a complex that seemed like housing for visiting university faculty. After we dropped the children off with X on Sunday, my mother said, "I think you should go look at that place that is being built up on the hill."

"Mom . . ." I felt defensive at both the gumption and indelicacy of her suggestion. "I can't afford it. You know that. What's the point in seeing it?"

But she forced me. To appease her, I walked up the steep private road to the property by myself, thinking, *What a friggin' waste of time.*

Carved into the mountain, the house was medium-sized, boxy, and irregular. Its windows gazed over the reservoir, and its personality was accentuated by the beetle-punctured boards that clad its walls, stained a dark red. A guy was moving dirt with an excavator when we walked up; he paused his work and explained that the owner was developing the site but didn't come in on Sundays, that the home wouldn't be ready until May or even June, and that it was completely eco-friendly, very efficient, built with recycled and salvaged materials.

"Oh." He stopped in his tracks. "And there he is!"

A very tall, broad-shouldered, slender man wearing shorts in the middle of Colorado January was strutting up the steep driveway, past the "For Sale" sign. We got introduced.

"Look, Michael," I said after we exchanged some basic information. "If for any reason you'd be interested in leasing this place to me with an option to buy, please give me a call."

"I hadn't considered that," he said, "but let me think about it."

I left him my number, as well as the contact details for the local real estate agent I had hired to find me a place, and made my way back down the hill. I told my mother, "The house will be very nice, and I met the builder. It's only for sale, though, so that's that."

"Well, you never know," she said.

I was about to board my flight back to New York when I got a call from my real estate agent. Surprised, I answered, "Doris?"

"Hey. Michael's agent just called me. He accepts your offer to lease the property with the option to buy. If you choose to move forward, he will lease you the house for $1,500 per month, $750 of which would go toward the down payment."

My heart was beating somewhere in my throat; this was a blessing that shone a bright ray into my reality. Later, I learned that Michael felt the same way: the house was his labor of love, but the market had tanked just as he was finishing it. I was his godsend as much as he was mine. On a routine weekend when neither of us expected anything, we had both gotten ourselves a deal that changed everything.

Within three months, the agreements that both Michael and I had with our agents ran out, and we ended up crafting an agreement directly between the two of us. I gave him $10,000—all the money in my possession—as the down payment, and he became my bank.

I talked to the owner of the bed-and-breakfast and secured a room for the few months until the house would be ready.

It was a very cold February day in New York when Ron asked to talk to me. Ron was, hands down, my landlord Craig's right-hand man. He ran the entire pier for him, acting as his property manager, head of security, and go-to person for anything that might need doing in Red Hook. And Ron took care of me: he picked up my mail and kept an eye on my place when I wasn't there. He was like a brother to me.

"Michelle, I know you love this place," he started. His tone was solemn; we were sitting in his truck while the chilling wind howled outside. "I know you spoke to Craig and you guys agreed to another nine years, same rate. But you are never here. Ever since you moved to California, then you won your battle, and now bought that new home in Colorado . . . You haven't been here in four months."

I had been running so hard, gliding across my reality, just an inch off denial, that I hadn't even noticed.

"Look," Ron continued, his words slow, deliberate, cognizant of their likely impact on me that day, "New York isn't going anywhere. And we will all be here when you are ready to come back."

I thanked him for his candor and respect, got out of the truck, and went back up to my space. I knew he was right; I had no idea how I was going to pay my Colorado mortgage on the random consulting jobs my schedule limited me to, let alone keep my Brooklyn pad. But I also sensed, deep enough to feel like knowing, that if I gave it up, I would never have a place like this—$5,200 per month for 10,000 square feet on the water, with the landlord that was like family to me—again.

Within another couple of weeks, Ron came by to see me again. "Can we talk for a minute?" he asked.

"Sure," I said.

"There is a kid running around, he's from the neighborhood and has just been funded his first million dollars. He's asked me to help find him a space." I was curious, but mostly about the punch line that was sure to come next. "It is up to you if you are going to let it go, but I wonder if your space may be perfect for him."

Who knows whether I would have given up my space had I not met "the kid." When he came by, I thought he was a delivery boy: young, hip, red hair, high-tops, freckles. And as he took in the possibilities of my space, I recognized that sparkle in his eyes. It had been in mine when I first walked in—the daring glare of potential, of being revved up to take over the world.

As he floated through the rooms, his ambition effortlessly

expanding to fill it, he told me about his company, Etsy, which was going to make homemade crafts accessible while offering a dignified living to their creators, many of whom were unable to work in the formal economy. He also told me about his grandma, who had raised him just around the corner in Red Hook, and about his best friend, now his employee, who was having a baby with his girlfriend.

"Would you be willing to sell your car?" he asked. "He could really use a car."

That's when I unmistakably recognized myself in him, looking after his people just as his world was about to change. There was nothing he couldn't accomplish, and I wouldn't be the one to stop that winning streak.

———

Another couple of weeks passed before I was able to see Craig.

"Hey, M!" he said. "Good to see you!"

"Hey!" I paused. "I met with the guy Ron mentioned was interested in my space, and I'm gonna give up my lease."

"Really?" Craig was surprised and concerned.

"Look, I just negotiated the lease for double what I was paying you, stipulating that you may put it up further in a year's time," I told him. "It's a great deal for you."

Craig, one of my angels, was finally going to be looked after the way he deserved, through a lease worthy of the place he and I had developed together. I had resolved that the sorrow I felt over leaving would be abated, at least in part, with the joy this deal would bring to him.

I would be out within a month, and was bereaving all that New York meant to me, when I had a surprise visit from Harris, Jackson's buddy and a core member of my formerly close-knit *And Baby* family. While he had sent no disparaging letters that I am aware of, I hadn't spoken to him since I shut down the magazine.

"Michelle . . ." The timidity and guilt in his voice were apparent. "I am sorry . . . I am so sorry. I could not begin to tell you how much I appreciate what you have done for me. I was angry and tried to make you responsible for my livelihood."

Of course, I held no grudge. I watched redemption begin to lift the yoke that had been weighing him down. Without me having to say a word about forgiveness, I watched him stand lighter, taller, look me bashfully in the eye. Apart from my industrious business controller, who sent me a touching letter many years later, he was the only one from *And Baby* to have reached out. I had not campaigned. I had not recruited righteous anger. *She needs them more than I do*—I had repeated that mantra in my head as I had witnessed them all, so malleable, turn away.

I had sold a car, the wood-burning stoves, and most of the office furnishings, including my gorgeous, ceiling-high trees, to Etsy, and the resulting check of $16,000-odd went to paying off the residual *And Baby* bills, my move, and several months of self-storage in New York.

When I stopped publishing *And Baby*, I had suspected that it wouldn't be too long before no one would notice it missing from the racks. And now, this was exactly how I felt about my life: all traces of me were being systematically erased.

———

Before my new home was ready, I had a couple more enriching visits from my family members. The first was from my brother, whose help at a time when I frequently felt exhausted was invaluable. After all, regardless of how elated I always was to see my children, they were five-year-old twins and could drain every ounce of energy from an able-bodied adult—even two. I also discovered a few unexpected saviors around town. Chuck E. Cheese's had an all-out game room that operated on tokens, and

FortFun, a local family entertainment center, could occupy the girls for hours. I became a regular there.

In parallel, I learned all I now know about the thirty-six princesses.

"Mama!" the girls would exclaim in frustrated disbelief when they wanted to role-play but I did not know the unabridged story of the Sleeping Beauty; alas, dolls had never been my thing. "We are the princess," they explained, gesturing to the elaborate outfits they would embellish with their imagination, "and you are the warrior."

The other visit was from my dear sister and her husband (Abudah), but once she traversed the geographical distance between us it only exacerbated how far apart we had grown. I had barely spoken to her since my split from X; because they had become inseparable with the children, they had stayed close to X and pulled away from me. I respected her choice, but especially after having been stripped bare and confined to near isolation, I missed her painfully.

They were in town for several days, while the girls were with X, and took the kids to Estes Park, a beautiful destination spot just a couple of hours from town. But I only saw my sister for ten minutes, when they dropped the children back off at the bed-and-breakfast at the beginning of my parenting time.

———

Next on the court-battle agenda were "at least three sessions of coparenting counseling with a licensed qualified mental health professional." I was surprised that X actually talked during these meetings, describing with quite a bit of enthusiasm how happy the children were in Colorado, and how much better their lives were now than they had ever been before—which would have been "with me."

The therapist's office was located in the historic area of

the downtown. She was white, obliging, and proper. And she seemed quite biased toward X, nodding fondly along with her statements while barely glancing in the direction of mine. In fact, she didn't even seem pro-gay, just pro-anger on behalf of victimized mommies.

To coincide with my parenting time, these sessions stretched over three months. But the time I actually spent with the twins during that time amounted to only a fraction of the hours I was supposed to have with my daughters, because X rarely released them promptly and sometimes didn't release them at all. Often when my scheduled parenting time arrived, X simply would not bring the children, or would not let them out of the house if I was picking them up. My calls to her would go unanswered, and, short of knocking on her door and making a scene that would surely unsettle the children, there was nothing I could do.

Finally, at one of the counseling sessions, I snapped.

"I do planes, trains, and automobiles to get here, drive through ice and snowstorms, and half the time she doesn't give me the kids!"

"Ms. Darné," the therapist said. Her selected tone was that of a vexed preschool teacher. "There is no reason for you to yell."

If I chose not to talk because I was afraid I would blow up, I also got dinged for not cooperating. But X appeared to exist in a space void of any expectations; no matter what she pulled, she was beyond reproach. I felt like rules and standards were ironclad and inexorable when directed at me, and yet sympathetic, malleable, and even ethereal where X was concerned. I was beginning to concede to the harsh truth that was growing more apparent, boisterous, and imperious with every interface I had with the legal system: whatever my plight, justice wasn't on offer.

Despite X's reference to my meeting Norma after the trial, that did not occur. I did meet her many months later, after the children had turned five, but it was purely by accident. By that point, the twins had started referring to her as Mom.

During one of my regular calls, X told me that the children would be performing in a ballet at the town's Lincoln Centre. I went straight there from my flight.

I was coming from San Francisco and had brought them beautiful music boxes, with delicate ballerinas spinning to mesmerizing classical music. I arrived ahead of the start time, and the girls ran to me the moment they spotted me. They were overtaken with thrill, not expecting to see me, and I was delighted to be there for them on the night of this momentous achievement.

As unlikely as it might seem, given that we had to buy tickets, my seat turned out to be a mere five or six rows behind X and her new partner. After the show, all of us ended up upstairs, at the celebration hosted by the performing company. Afterward, I walked the children to their car and buckled them into their seats, all to the sound of their jubilant chatter.

"You must be Norma?" I said, through the passenger's window, to the woman in the driver's seat. I was happy for the children and wanted to extend an invitation to start fresh in our coparenting relationship. I smiled. "Or, I guess I should call you Mom?"

Norma said nothing and barely made eye contact, exhibiting no respect or courteousness befitting the situation. I kissed my babies good-bye and left.

I chose to pick my battles and focused my energy on solidifying my parenting arrangement. With the temporary parenting agreement timidly guarding my rights, we started negotiating a long-term plan that became known as the Global Agreement. It built on initial insight collected by my attorneys while X was still living in Florida, and it mostly represented a series of concessions from me as I, fatigued, came to surrender more and more of my ground. But we were on a path to an agreement that was better than the temporary one, and I believed that whatever I didn't get on the first go I could revisit once we stabilized.

In the meantime, June was approaching, and so was the time for me and the girls to move into our new home. I didn't have enough cash, so I grudgingly borrowed what I needed from a close friend. I hired movers to pick up the furnishings of both the Pennsylvania house and the Brooklyn office from my New York storage space and then drive to California, where I met them at the storage facility that primarily housed the belongings X had left behind when she went to Florida, and then finally to Colorado.

It was Thursday, June 15, 2008, and I arrived at my Colorado property full of clashing emotions. A couple of guys were hurriedly pounding the finishing touches into our new home. Within a couple of hours, the moving truck arrived and unloaded everything. The children were coming in two days, so that was all the time I had to filter through several discontinued lifetimes and set up the home for our future.

I involved the girls in making the new house truly our own. We sat amid dozens of floor tiles while they picked out their favorites, a process that resulted in our bathroom floors being undeniably and randomly colorful.

"We have three options," Michael advised me and the children as we considered our recycled carpet options. Michael had already convinced me—and it had taken some effort—that I did not want to endure Colorado winters with hardwood floors in the bedrooms. He tabled a near-white option I was unashamedly eyeing and picked up a different sample. "I recommend this one; its mix of pigments will help hide the red dirt we have around here."

Really? I thought, a little dismayed.

"We agree, mama! This one is best!"

Bummer. I was overpowered three to one.

"We want this one!"

So the speckled taupe won over the white, and my girls were very proud of themselves.

"This is our home. It was built with love," I would tell them. And it was. Michael had built it for his own family, crafting every piece of joinery for their use. My luck came when his family voted against moving to the mountains. However, the original, love-steeped intention of the home was with us every day—as were the proportions: Michael is six foot four, so I struggled to see anything but sky out of any of our windows and required a stepstool to reach kitchen cupboards. "I never thought I'd be selling my house to such a shorty," was all the compassion Michael had to offer.

At some point, proud of their design contribution and keen to show off their room, the girls brought X up to the house. Their excited "Mommy, look!" echoed throughout the house as they showed her all around.

X appeared to grow uneasy. "This is our old furniture," she said to me in a tone of either a surprise or an epiphany. "I have to go now," she said to the girls, and she left more abruptly than they had expected.

———

"Are we going to that non-proper house on the hill?" Juliette's question startled me when I next picked the girls up.

"Yes, that house on the hill is our home, and we are going there, yes."

Over the following weeks, I was repeatedly confronted with similar comments. One weekend, I finally snapped. "What isn't proper about it?"

"Well, you know. It just *isn't*, Mama," was the response, delivered in a tone of reproach.

"No, I *don't* know. Tell me. Has it not got enough room for you to play?" I asked sarcastically, since we had an acre. The children just stared. "Has it got too many stairs—or not enough?" *Or is it simply because it is mine?*

They could never explain, and I didn't truly expect them to. *Proper* isn't a word that five-year-olds use much.

———

Often, when I arrived for my scheduled parenting time, X simply would not let the children out of her house and I would wait, curbside, for hours in a silent, ineffectual protest until the door would finally open and they would run toward my car.

My daughters were barely five, and now that I was living nearby, their excitement over seeing me again after so many months apart had worn off. Now, when I did spend time with them, exhausted and heartbroken, they often treated me terribly, parroting anger and distortions they could only have picked up in X's household.

"*Bad* Mama!" An insolent five-year-old would stare me down with condemnation if I got caught smoking, or packing something they didn't want into their lunchbox, or demonstrating my inadequacy in any other way.

"Why did you sue Mommy?" Juliette would ask questions that were oversize for her mind, furious from the second I picked them up. X must have complained to them about court. "How could you do this to us, to our family? How *could* you, Mama?"

Her aggression would put me right back on the stand where I had clamored to legitimize my own existence. This time, the prosecutor was my five-year-old daughter, who couldn't possibly know that the weight of adult issues was cutting her childhood short.

———

Cobalt blue. Auburn. Slate gray. Blending into each other. Taupe. Mauve. Indigo. These were the colors of my Sunday evenings after the children left my house; such were the hues of my bathroom floor tiles blurring together, veiled by the tears in my eyes.

The thumping of my heavy steps, resonating through an empty, hardwood house. The gushing of my bathwater. The unstoppable tears. Distress calls escaping through sobs. These were the sounds of my Sunday evenings. Despair would tunnel into me, burrowing through my resolve, voiding my path, fragmenting who I knew myself to be. My yearning, muted. My strength coiled into fetal position. My expansive presence reduced to mere millimeters between punctuation within legal documents. My commitment to provide for my family recast as a cover for abandoning them. My resolve to soar interpreted as naked ambition. *When this is done, will there be any of me left?* Hollow and bereft, I wondered.

One Sunday in particular, Alyssa's voice overpowered all other thoughts. "If you hadn't sued Mommy, if you had just been nice, you could have just had us whenever you wanted."

I cried myself to sleep nearly every night, but I continued to shrug off the frequent advice to give up, dished out by those friends and colleagues who did not have children and could not comprehend why I would continue to torture myself, why I would choose to ruin my life.

———

"Hey," X said one day when I called for the children. "They are treating Norma really bad."

"Our kids?!" I did not expect this of them.

"Yes. They are really mean to her. They are making her feel like there is nothing she can do right simply because she is not you. For example, she'll mention that she wants to buy a motorcycle, and they'll mock her, saying, 'Oh, our mama surfs!'"

"I'll talk to them."

I was true to my word. That weekend, I found a minute to talk to them.

"Guys, listen up!"

Two strong-willed faces turned my way, at attention.

"I know that Norma is new to you; I know you do not like that Mommy and I do not live in the same house anymore. But Norma cares for you, and she is an adult who you need to treat with respect. Do you understand?"

Two heads bobbed.

"Please try to treat her nice; give her a chance to show you how much she loves you. Promise me?"

More nodding.

During another weekend at the house, I heard Juliette exclaim, "No, Mommy!" while she was on the phone with X.

Her resolute verdict startled me out of cooking dinner. I walked over to her just as she slammed the phone down. "Did you just hang up on Mommy?"

"Yes I did!"

At five, she was remarkably aware of her boundaries and already independent enough to cut off her main caretaker. There was no doubt that Mommy was going to be served a handful in the coming years.

"I don't want to speak with her!" Juliette said, her little body defiant and her tone ferocious.

"Don't you hang up on your mother! Call her right back and apologize."

"You just don't know how it is, Mama! You don't understand!" Juliette was furious.

"Listen to me!" I kneeled right on the floor in front of her and put my hands on her face to get her attention. "No matter how she may make you feel at times, she is your mother, and you must respect her."

After a few more rounds of the tantrum, Juliette called X back and apologized. I was proud of her, even if the affirmation of parental roles was never to be mutual.

The agreement we were negotiating allowed me to make up time if I couldn't get to Colorado due to inclement weather, or if I fell sick. One time, I had been sick for a week, hoping to get better by the time I was scheduled to fly, by the time my mother insisted that I see our family doctor. I called the practice I had been going to my hole life. The head-doctor's daughter picked up the phone and said, "I got it; no need for an appointment, just come in, Michelle."

The doctor had bad news. "You have bronchial pneumonia. A bad case of it. I am very sorry, but you absolutely have to rest, and categorically no flying for ten days."

I texted X from the doctor's office, explaining why I had to reschedule my time and informing her that I was on my way to FedEx to send her the doctor's note. I got her return text while driving; it read, "You are lying. I called the doctor's office and they didn't have an appointment for you."

The next day, so much for bed rest, I drove back to the doctor and begged him, embarrassed, to write a note explaining the situation. Upon receiving the scan I sent, X replied that I had forged the note.

Whenever I have been sick or delayed since, X has always made it absolutely clear that rescheduling isn't an option. However, another time stands out for a different reason. I was in the Bay Area and really sick but had a project starting in just a few days in LA. So I stocked up on tissues and ibuprofen and flew to LA a couple of days early to allow myself time to get better.

One of my dear friends was also traveling to LA and flew with me, which was of great help since I felt absolutely awful.

"Hey, M, I think that woman likes you!" My friend teased me at the boarding gate.

Until she pointed it out, I hadn't even noticed that I was being stared at. The woman looked kind of familiar, but my congested head could not give me more than that.

The next time I spoke to the children, Alyssa flooded me with unexpectedly accusatory questions. "Mama, why didn't you pick us up? We waited for you, why didn't you? Mommy said you chose to work rather than be with us, why would you do that?"

Just when I felt my tenuous position with the children could not get any worse, X had surprised me again.

"Bean, listen to me," I implored. "That is not what happened." I explained the situation.

"But, Mama . . ." The hope in Alyssa's voice was so bottomless, so vast it could have filled an ocean. "Mommy would never lie to me, would she?"

"Oh, honey." Once again, I bit my tongue and did my job as a parent of a five-year-old. "You know, sometimes people get very angry and they say things they don't mean. Perhaps Mommy is just really angry with me." I made it okay for them, again, all the while wondering what motivates people to stick their noses into other people's lives.

I had accepted that my ex-wife was going to turn our children against me every chance she got. But I could not believe the snitching. I had finally placed that woman from the airport: both she and her husband used to work for *And Baby*. I had given them opportunities and signed their checks; I had hired her niece because she really wanted to move to New York; and I had written a personal check for $5,000, instructing Josh to find an apartment for this young lady, after she had moved on from us but was about to end up on the street. However, when her aunt saw me at the airport, and with another woman, she felt entitled to inform X about it.

"There is nothing you can do without me finding out—nothing," was my ex-wife's comment on how she came about the information she had used with the children for additional leverage in vilifying me.

The battle against me raged on all fronts: the legal system, my children's disdain for me, and my ex-wife's masterful spin. On top of that, I was fighting for financial survival. I was under no illusion that I would be granted a dispensation, let alone empathy, should I not be able to afford to travel to see the kids.

CHAPTER 9:
SIDELINED

ANGUISH: excruciating or acute distress, suffering, or pain.

By the end of the summer, I was celebrating a warped milestone, measured by how much I had relented more than by how much had been achieved. After nine months, X and I had finally landed on an acceptable version of the Global Agreement.

While I would have loved to have unlimited time with my children, which realistically could be no more than 50 percent of the time, it was not to be. Our life would be restricted to two blips of Thursday night to Sunday. I fought on for consecutive weekends because I felt that week-to-week rotations would be disruptive to children at that age, and because consecutive time would allow me more uninterrupted time to earn a living. My attorney did relay to me that X met any mention of my work with grandstanding and palpable disdain, but I pushed through. I didn't have the option of collecting child support.

I would be but "permitted visitation." My role hung by its teeth while X would "retain 100 percent sole physical custody" even while we shared "joint legal custody."

In September 2008, I would have the children from 3:30 p.m. on Wednesday through 8:00 a.m. on Sunday morning. Every month I would pick up an extra day, and by December 2008 they would be with me for a continuous week, interrupted only by one night—Wednesday—spent with X. This was all I could get for now, but my intention was to go back to court once the children were less dependent on primary care—a consideration of continuity that was critically important both to me and to the family court system—and keep picking up days until their lives were equally facilitated between two households.

"I don't fuckin' agree with either one of you!" John had said about this logic to me and Ann. "Get 50 percent now, or you will never get it! Take the crumbs, and she will always treat you as less-than; you will never recover!"

But I respected the needs befitting the children's age and trusted the system, so I didn't listen. Most people don't need a contract to parent by, and I'm pretty sure nobody would expect the well-being of their children to hinge on a pronoun; well, neither did I.

Ludicrous even in 2008, I had to provide X with the travel itinerary "no less than 90 days prior to the intended vacation time" if I wished to take the girls anywhere for one of two, strictly non-consecutive, weeks of vacation I was allowed with them. Which was the only time they were permitted to leave town with me.

Furthermore, I would be "entitled to talk with the children on the telephone on any Sunday or Thursday when [I did] not have visitation," and we would alternate custody of the children for the Mother's Day weekend. Mine would fall on even years.

Based on declared income, the child support required of me would start at $1,019 per month (while the children were with me 11.66 percent of the time) and drop to $911 per month starting December 2008, once I had them for "week-long visits" that amounted to 23.58 percent of the time.

The only thing I pushed back against was unlimited education expenses. I was going to agree to it, but my attorney got insistent and this time I listened to reason. I would have a say, presumably alongside the children by that point, in how much we could afford to pay for their higher education.

Having gulped up about $100,000 in legal fees for me, these were the most expensive three and a half pages of my life—and still they tossed me mere scraps of time to parent my children, all the while denigrating it as nothing more than "visitation." Nevertheless, I was satisfied. We were moving past the divorce, my time was secure, and I would figure out how to do my job within the little allotment that it was.

On September 20, 2008, X signed and notarized the Global Agreement in Colorado.

We reconvened in court, where the judge would motion to file our Global Agreement. My attorney presented the executed agreement for the judge's consideration but flagged an issue. "Judge, the agreement has been executed. However, the document that was sent to this court, as well as to me, was a copy, and we need the original in order to file."

"Oh, I am sorry, I didn't realize that." On speaker, X sounded both apologetic and agreeable. "I will get the original sent to you right away."

The judge acknowledged her promise with a nod. "This court hereby orders that the original executed copy be submitted, which will at that point be accepted as the effective stipulated order on file with this court."

Administrative logistics notwithstanding, we were done. I thanked and released my attorneys.

———

Whenever we spoke in the weeks that followed, I asked X whether she had sent the original to the court. "Oh, I sent it," was the response I got several times. But it never arrived. Then, when I pushed, she started making references to money. "You'll get it when you pay all that money you owe me," she said. I suspected she was referring to the unconfirmed amount of back child support I was repaying monthly, but it was hard to be sure. I just knew it couldn't be good.

Once more, I wasn't sure how solid the ground I walked on was, and it chipped away at what otherwise was taking on the contours of stability with the children. In December, I finally had the girls for a whole week and used the rest of the time to ramp up my efforts at work. Christmas was approaching—our first Christmas at the new house—and I was excited.

Somewhere, I found contact details for "Santa." We could e-mail him, or, for just a few bucks, the girls could reach the voice mail of "Santa's workshop." The girls were giddy excited and insisted that we do both, just to leave nothing to chance.

"Hello? Santa Claus?" Pause. My darling girl was perched, all nerves, at the gossip table I had brought from Pennsylvania as she listened to the recording. I watched her gather up all the professionalism she had observed in her life into well-formed, measured words vital to her hopes for toys.

"We'll be at Mama's house, not Mommy's house!" Juliette said, wrapping up the call with commanding directions about altering Santa's usual drop-off route. "Mama's house."

To this day, I can't help smiling every time I think how gorgeous it must be to listen to those messages. I hope somebody did. Hey, I wish we all could, as there is nothing quite like pure, unwavering faith in magic.

Alyssa was hovering next to her, anxiously waiting for her turn to call. "Hi, Santa . . . It's Alyssa," she finally uttered. "Oh, and . . . and I'll be at Mama's house, too." As befitting her personality, she spoke more quietly and with greater reticence than her sister. It was only afterward, when she kept asking me whether I thought Santa had heard her, whether he knew she had been good, whether I was sure he was going to try to get her what she asked for—relentless, precious, heartwarming inquisition—that the intensity of her personality came through again.

As the holidays approached, I nested joy in my anticipation of the girls' laughter, like jingle bells, and in the nurturing company of my parents, who would be joining us in Colorado.

When she arrived, my mother dressed our home in Christmas spirit, tasteful decorations, and a pile of deliciously wrapped gifts waiting for the children to arrive.

Two days before Christmas Eve, I was on the phone with X.

"You would be lucky if I dropped them off because you are two months late on child support," she said.

"X!" Her name escaped, a wail in response to this brutal, unexpected wound, through my tears. "Please! Please don't do this now . . . I am trying the best I can to pay you, working my ass off to keep up."

"Come January, we are going back to the original order until you catch up your child support."

"You can't do this! I am legitimately their other parent, I won my case!"

"What you won," X said, sounding cunning and sarcastic, "is the right to pay for them. And nothing more."

Her words, so cruel, mauled me. They infected my soul, leaching deep into the fibers of my subconscious, hijacking my dreams into nightmares. Truth was whatever she needed it to be.

"Please . . ." I felt smaller than the phone I held to my ear. "My parents are here, X!"

When X dropped the children off on Christmas Eve, they ran straight into the outstretched arms of their beloved grandparents. Umpa acted like a playful, unaffected bear, but I saw his eyes glisten. He had not seen them in two and a half years. Ummie could not have been happier. "Oh, my goodness!" she cried. "You are so, so big!"

The girls visibly basked in that pride.

I remember my father sitting in the armchair by the front door. X brought him a six-pack of beer that was his namesake, explaining excitedly that it was from a local brewery.

I brought myself to address her, still believing we could leave bitterness behind. It was Christmas, after all. "Hey," I said, "why don't you and Norma join us tomorrow for the Christmas meal? The kids would love that."

X shrugged it off; they never came.

———

X did indeed singlehandedly revert to the temporary agreement after December. She denied me any access to the children beyond the meager weekend hours I had been afforded over the previous year. Too often, I would wait, curbside, for hours, only to return home without my children. Always combating that inexplicable anxiety, I lived in a constant state of thirst for them. I needed to take X back to court, but I could not reengage my attorneys because I was still paying them off. So for months, perhaps a year, her rage ran rampant across my life, reaching much farther than could ever be justified in a coparenting situation.

Of course, the children did not understand the legalities involved. They just knew that Mama was not there when they expected her to be, and because I didn't like to throw their Mommy under the bus, they got used to assuming it was my fault.

I was dashing around like mad—compelling clients to give me business, rebooking airfares, wielding creative solutions, instilling confidence, tucking the girls in by phone, renting cars, warding off debtors, handling X's underhanded e-mails, playing Maleficent, facing judges, compelling clients . . .

I liked the colors of the trees outside but could not distinguish one season from another. Colleagues and acquaintances opened their mouths, but the words that came out were muted. News anchors spoke too fast for me to capture their meaning.

When had Despair been stamped in my life passport? Why had it gone right over Love and distorted Justice beyond recognition? And how could I find a place to connect to these other people not living my life?

———

In 2009, I finally did what my corporate attorneys had advised me to do in 2006. Crushed and humiliated, I filed for bankruptcy.

X was automatically notified, and she confronted me the next time we spoke. "Is this how you take care of things?" she demanded. "Go bankrupt? Let all your investors down?"

Years earlier, she had taken me to dinner because Josh needed to talk to me about something. The tactic seemed way too complex for my busy head, but of course I went.

"Josh is really struggling," she opened that evening. "I think he needs to declare bankruptcy, but the only one who can make it okay for him is you. He is embarrassed out of his mind. Please, talk to him."

I did. I even gave him the money for a bankruptcy attorney.

Mere weeks after I went bankrupt, so did my ex-wife's beloved aunt. But it was only me who bore the mark of utter failure for exercising, however hesitantly, this right of every American citizen.

"Don't you dare," might have been what I mustered in response to X.

———

Even as our new home adopted its disparate furnishings and their varied history, one box had remained unpacked. Marked "Jackson," it held the toys, scarves, and other belongings that were awaiting her move to Colorado, but I was now doubting whether it was such a good idea. She was getting older, and the eleven-hour trip from New York, inclusive of quarantine on both sides, would take a toll on her. On top of that, I was gone traveling constantly and had nobody in Colorado who could take care of her so that I didn't have to board her. At least in Brooklyn she was living with Harris, her devout best friend. So at some point, I sent the box back to New York.

I would never see Jackson again.

That first time I held my daughters, vowing that I would sacrifice anything for them, I had no idea that the sacrifice required of me would be so prolific and incessant.

Summer was approaching, and I decided to take the children to California. They hadn't seen most of their family since they were three and didn't even remember some of them. Plus, I was depleted beyond measure; having my parents and sisters around would ensure that the girls had a fantastic time, regardless of my ability to keep up with them.

I notified X of my plan.

"I have already spoken with DCS [Department of Child Services], and if you have not paid your child support, they will have the authority to pick you up at the airport," she told me. "I will have them waiting for you, you will not be able to get on that flight, and they will bring the children home to me."

That would have been devastating, never mind scary, for the children, and I was not willing to put them through that. So I backed down, unaware—and too distraught to even consider—that she was bluffing. Later I realized that since the case was in California, she would not have been able to make good on her threat. For now, though, I simply assured myself that we would go another time and notified her of the change of plans.

I hadn't seen the kids since that exchange until I pulled up to X's house a couple of weeks later for pickup.

"Mama, are we going to California?" they asked me, all excited jitters.

I did my best to keep my dumbfounded silence from spilling into the car. "Well, no. Not this time"—I heard the first sob—"but another time for sure."

"Oh, you're not taking them to California?" I heard X's voice, believably surprised, and turned my head to see her leaning assuredly into the open passenger seat window. "That's a shame. The kids were so excited to go."

The backseat was engulfed in tears, and nothing but disappointment and blame was directed at me all the way up the mountain as I drove to our "improper" house.

Even though disappointment took a while to wear off for each of us, we spent our vacation week between the house and the lake, playing with make-believe characters in the mud and building forts from blankets.

———

At some point, pained watching me struggle, my nephew said, "Come on, Aunt Shell; you are representing yourself in court, and she is walking all over you. You need to get help. I know this paralegal; she is really, really good and *way* less expensive than a lawyer."

That was how I met Sue.

"I can't get my ex-wife to adhere to the parenting agreement we negotiated, but I let my attorneys go when it was executed. Can you help with this?" I asked her.

Sue had been a paralegal in Contra Costa County for some twenty-five years, helping many people who, like me, could not afford attorney fees. Experienced, thorough, and diligent, she was well respected in the California court system. I needed her to say yes, and she did.

Sue proceeded to help me package my case for what turned out to be four more different judges. Ours was the last case that Judge Baskins presided over prior to his retirement after twenty years on the bench, and until his position was duly filled, various judges were temporarily assigned to it. Furthermore, every time help seemed possible, it was intercepted by X filing for a change of venue. She tirelessly resubmitted her arguments, among which was the complaint that Colorado gave children a voice by putting them on the stand earlier than did California.

The court personnel had coined our case "the bitter divorce," and I understand why the transient judges handled it like a hot potato. Given the case's complexity, they required detailed briefing on every matter but ended up offering little more than caution in return. However, the court's inaction was permitting X to undercut my relationship with our children, and my ability to parent them, even when her claim against my rights failed.

At one point, Sue yelled on the phone, "What the hell is going on there? I cannot believe these things keep happening to you!"

I would take whatever I could get, and with one of the judges, it was mere enforcement of common sense before she moved on to the next case.

"Ms. Darné, it is valiant of you to pay for your children's extracurricular activities. However, note that you do not have to. Ms. X, did you hear that?"

My ex-wife was quiet on the phone, so the judge had to repeat herself.

"Ms. X, did you catch that Ms. Darné is in no way obligated to extend funds beyond those stipulated for child support?"

"Fine," was X's response.

One of the latter judges echoed my dismay regarding the entire situation. "You are two very smart women," she said, firmly but respectfully. "This court is not here to raise your children. It is not this court's responsibility to make decisions about your parenting; that is your responsibility."

I supposedly owed X stacks of money, and as such was not worthy of seeing our children, despite the fact that the system vehemently disconnects one from the other (not to mention the fact that nobody could tell me what, exactly, I owed). Since I was paying X directly, the process required her receipts before my liability was adjusted. I also continued to pay half of the fees for the various activities our children participated in, but that did not count toward anything.

"Michelle, you need to go back to court," Sue advised. "This money thing is giving X way too much power over you. And you should not be paying her directly; you should be paying into the system."

Until that moment, I hadn't even known that was an option. That summer, the summer of 2009, I filed to establish a firm basis of child support for our family.

Child support denoted a whole separate system; it had its own court and its own judges. The day I went in, on September 16, 2009, I was the only woman among thirty parents. The twenty-nine fathers present were respondents, meaning they had to come. Some fought their obligation to pay, others had attempted to leverage money to demand time with their children, and many had been denied visitation even though they did pay. Out of the thirty of us, I was the only person who was there of her own free will.

A number of factors are taken into account when setting the amount of monthly child support owed: the expenses involved in raising the children, their specific needs, and the incomes of the two parents. X, who had the ability to earn six-figure salaries, declared an average monthly income of $798 per month.

"I am sorry, Ms. Darné, your attorney was correct," the child support judge told me. "Nothing you have given to X can be counted toward what you owe." I had already heard this from Judge Baskins. The over $20,000 that I had given to X across ten months wasn't acknowledged. Ten percent interest was, however, tacked on in arrears.

After my case was heard, the judge moved on to the next one. I waited in the back to collect my paperwork. I saw it being brought to the judge for approval, but, after a brief glance, she motioned it back and went on with the current case. The next time it made its way to her, a couple more cases later, she looked up and raised her hand to signal a pause.

"Please excuse me. Officers in the back, you need to hear me. This paperwork is wrong, again; this is three times now. Yes, Ms. Darné owes back child support. But she is also the one who filed this case. She is the petitioner, not the respondent."

Two and a half hours later, the bias was finally stripped from my paperwork, which plainly stated that I owed $34,998.37 in back child support, inclusive of $2,931.37 in interest. I would pay $250 toward it every month, in addition to the regular child support set at $1,250 per month.

At least I now knew where I stood. And I could care for our children—with funds if not with time, as the latter was never on my side.

———

"What is my job?" I would often ask the girls, lightly masking my playfulness with a serious tone.

"To teach us to fly!" Four little arms would extend up and out and catch an upward current into a twirl, faces gleaming. Their wings lifted my weary heart into the sun, their self-absorbed delight paring away the gloom I was carrying around.

Another two of my most fond memories also date back to those times.

I was in the kitchen with Juliette when she said, "Mama, you've worked really hard to be with us, haven't you?"

I don't remember how I responded, but I was taken by complete surprise and rendered at once vindicated, forgiven, and defenseless.

"Mama!" Alyssa called out on another day while leading me up our stairs to the second floor. "You know," she said, her voice filled with pride, "I really like you!" The moment wrapped around me like a plush cashmere throw. I wanted to crawl under those words, to inhabit their validation of my struggles, and to hold on to that look in her eyes, to bottle it like precious essence.

Amidst the devastation that swept through my life, hope glistened in these rare moments when my children were not punishing me for what they thought I had done. And my spirit was revived when pure strangers and true friends extended life-saving kindnesses that enabled me to create a new and nurturing home for my family in Colorado.

Any dreams or ambitions put aside, I juggled the choices X was leaving for me—which, as long as I continued to choose my children, were very few. I was turning down positions that would have paid $550,000 per year but were incompatible with my schedule, and I was manifesting silver linings where I could. For example, since I could not see the children in the first week of the month, I consoled myself that this gave me a chance to start the month off at my office in California.

But I was hemorrhaging money and every month running a high risk of spending a week at an empty Colorado house, should my ex-wife feel vindictive.

"Why don't you get a job?" she asked me one day, chipping in, looting in on my struggles. "Or are you too used to living on investors' money?"

X had opened a child support case in the state of Colorado in early 2009—never mind that she was not supposed to, since we had an active case in California. By the time the incessant—and demeaning—phone calls and letters from the Colorado case workers started pouring in, it appeared they had been enlisted in a crusade to vindicate a mother (X) abandoned by a no-good, very bad, deadbeat father (me).

The following spring I received a letter dated April 21, 2010, that read:

"Dear Ms. Darne:"

(They couldn't even bother to get my name—or punctuation—right.)

"I have received the copies of checks/receipts you sent for proof of child support payment. The check from First Republic Bank . . . dated 11/14/18 is clearly made payable to X, but there is no reference on this check stating that it is for child support."

Why else would I be sending my ex-wife money after she has put me through hell? A morning-tea book club gathering?!

"The same is true of the check from WAMU," the letter went on, "dated 10/3/08 in the amount of $1582.00, which is made payable to X . . . Cannot be verified as child support without a receipt from Ms. X . . . The same is true of the receipt . . . there is no legible date . . . Again, Ms. X would have to acknowledge that she received cash from you on that date, which was not reported in her arrears affidavit of 10/27/09.

"If she agrees, then the money will be deducted from the arrears due we are showing on this case. If she disagrees, then you two will need to go to court to obtain a ruling by the judge . . . It is your attorney's interpretation of the guidelines in which he believes that the child support should be decreased to $911. Your child support order dated 9/24/09 calls for $1,250.00 per month . . . This order makes no mention of the Declaration provided 5/8/08."

Of course, I thought. Having sent that Trojan Horse of a copy, X had never gotten around to filing the original executed Global Agreement.

The calls were worse than the letters. I had never felt so diminished, so judged, by the person on the other end of the phone. I was a liar. Deadbeat parents like me belonged in jail.

Pride shed, spirit peeled raw, I obediently jumped through hoops and sat for a treat, resubmitting receipts and waiting for

X to agree. Both Sue and the California child support officer assigned to my case advised me to do no such thing; my case was *not* in Colorado, they told me, and under no pretenses was I to pay any money there.

On May 10, 2010, a fresh letter came from DHS.

"As you will note, Ms. X has given you credit for the cash payments in September, 2008. She has also given you credit for cash payments in the amount of $4,400.00 in January, 2009. Although she maintains she never received the money orders, she has given you credit of $3,476.00."

My ex-wife's mysterious grace toward me was searing.

"Accordingly we have given you credit for that amount against the arrears due. As stated in the letter sent to you on 4/21/10, the court order we are enforcing is for $1,250 per month. It is imperative that you make payment soon on this case as automatic enforcement actions will be taken. Your arrears on this case are $24,297.00. Thank you for your cooperation on this matter." Signed, Dianne. Legal Technician/Paralegal.

"I told you, Shelly!" my mom countered. "It has always been just about the money for her. How many times do you need me to tell you that she's no good before you listen to me? Before you see her for who she really is?"

It is magical how the spirit can shield itself from truths that may crush it—how the mind can rearrange incongruent information until it constructs a reality it can accept. Many, many more times, Mom.

I was there that weekend in Pennsylvania when my mother recognized X for somebody very different than the woman I thought I was marrying. In the years that followed, my mother admitted X into our family; she heeded the sentiment of X's apology, respected my choice, and adored her grandchildren. But never again did she truly trust my ex-wife.

When X cut me out, my mother sent her a letter. I have never seen it, but X, when we were still talking, told me about it and admitted that it had been tough to swallow. My mother had accused her of lying to her; of taking the children; of betraying me and the family, despite how well they had treated her.

———

Back at my parents' house, I was beat. I felt like my ex-wife had me exactly where she wanted me: untraceably compromised and but an accidental nudge away from the primed crescendo, one in which I would be defeated, broke, back on drugs, and on the street. Not that any of that would be reason enough to waive my child support obligation.

My mother and I were standing at the kitchen island—me crying, her once again soothing me—when my father walked in through the garage door and saw me.

"Come on, champ!" he said. "You're knocked down but not knocked out. Get back up! Fight!"

"Dad!" My plea ripped the air. I was an exposed nerve floating among obstructions, my experience purely visceral, worn out by venom, my defenses so ineffectual that I felt as if a single word could break my skin, one look could disassemble what was left of me. "Don't you think I know this?!" Sobs were bursting out, scratching my voice raw. "I'm beat. Can you just, this once, not be my coach and please just be my father!"

My father froze up for a few moments before his fighting stance morphed into a couple of shuffled steps toward me. Then he wrapped me up in his arms and kissed my head as I bawled into his chest.

Although I wished my dad hadn't pushed me that night, I did understand why he did. Ever since it saved his own life, sport—along with its vocabulary and metaphors—had been a key coping mechanism for our whole family. My father grew up utterly neglected by his mother (and her various husbands and lovers), left alone for weeks at a time from his early primary school years. Often hungry for days, he learned how not to waste a scrap, all the while hiding below the radar of Child Protective Services. By the time he was in middle school, he was practically living at a boxing gym run by his uncles, who were professional fighters; their pictures still adorn his bedroom walls. The world of sport, its demand for commitment, its emphasis on honor, and its celebration of individual tenacity and achievement set the tone for his life. Sport was his ultimate welder of character, and character was his ultimate trophy.

When I was growing up, my parents made sure to live in all-white neighborhoods because they were determined that I would not grow up limited by the color of my skin. However, I would often run home crying because other kids called me a negro—that is, until my father took me to the punching bag and started teaching me to fight rather than let me demean myself with my anger. And whatever sport I played, my father was always there, standing in the rain or the scorching sun, supporting, watching, and reminding me that my toughest coach didn't wear the team jersey. My dad didn't miss any weakness or any mistake, and while he didn't say much, his look of disapproval stung worse than losing. So I played harder, better, through pain and despite childhood fears, to avoid that look.

But nothing could have prepared me for having my existence annulled by the person I married. I was getting decimated while fighting honorably in what was essentially a cage fight. Still, that was the only way I could react, even if it killed me; it was what he had taught me, and the only way for me to live with myself.

———

When it became evident that we were not getting any traction, Sue gave me a talk, her voice kind and urgent. "Michelle, I cannot believe the judges, one after the other, will not make X live by the agreement she had executed. I hate to say this, but I think you need more than I can offer; you need an attorney."

I had to agree with her. Accepting that my ex-wife might actually be intent on purging me out of my children's lives, I engaged an attorney named Rebecca.

Since X had stopped adhering to the Global Agreement, over two years of our lives had passed. Twice, the courtroom had been cleared for our case—an extreme measure given the court's packed schedule. Countless rations of sixty-three hours had been trespassed and undermined by the time I filed a new motion to modify custody and visitation in April 2010 and, soon after, stood before Judge Scanlon in court.

"So." We had seen her a few times by this point, and Judge Scanlon spoke in a stoic voice hardened by years of resolving unbearable betrayals of the family unit. "I understand that there are two different agreements out there. However, we only have one here in court." She was acknowledging the original, temporary agreement issued in early 2008. However, when it came to the second one, don't be fooled; she wasn't referring to the Global Agreement. By that stage, X and her attorney had written up a whole new parenting agreement, which was represented as an agreement I had consented to, and which, allegedly, I was now "arbitrarily" refusing to sign. My mind felt like a spring, wound up to the point of snapping, demanding release.

"Ms. Darné won't sign this agreement," X's attorney pronounced in court.

My court battles usually left me feeling mutilated and baffled, but on this occasion a wave of anger rose through me. The very existence of the Global Agreement that I had fought so hard for had been erased from the court's collective memory.

I lost it.

"I don't understand this!" My voice was amplified; my gestures were incomplete and anxious. "I have a new judge, the fifth judge so far, and that's fine. But I keep trying to get you to hear me, and you just won't! We negotiated and executed our agreement, the Global Agreement, but X has never submitted the original despite the orders of this court. Why does this keep happening? Why can't anybody make her comply with this court's orders?"

"Ms. Darné!" Judge Scanlon sounded appalled. I was exactly who my ex-wife had meticulously set me up to become: a volatile Latina erupting in fury at a respectable judge. "Calm down, or you'll be deemed to be in contempt of court!"

The bailiff had already stood up from his seat and was leaning forward with ready enforcement arms folded.

The dirty, conniving lash of injustice floored me—cast down, throbbing, and shamed. What I heard in the judge's response was, "You raised your voice at me, you worthless parent!" Her judgment spilled into the cacophony of ridicule already looping in my mind, spouted by other civil servants, counselors, and former colleagues who seemed mesmerized by my ex-wife's impassioned campaign against me.

You! The cunning aggressor of good Catholic girls! You! The bully of delicate mothers! I could hear their chanting echo inside my head, their allegations nothing but excuses to disregard what I may have to say. "If I don't like *how* you said it, I don't have to hear it." How convenient. The ultimate act of privilege, even though most who exercise it would be shocked to hear that they abuse power. A socially acceptable way out of assuming any responsibility. Including the responsibility for having picked, and picked, and prodded you, your flesh already raw; your grace already depleted; your dignity butchered, no longer a source of endurance.

"In light of persistent disagreement between the parties . . ."

Silenced, I watched the lips of the judge as she negated the last four years of my life.

". . . this court orders that Ms. X and Ms. Darné return to mediation with the objective of reaching a new parenting agreement."

Back to square one.

"This court is adjourned."

FUCK! X won, again. Will she ever let our children settle into a secure and stable life across two households?

I felt as if I had somehow, in a moment I could not recall, opted for an awake, open-heart surgery and woken up on the operating table—immobilized but not anesthetized—just in time to feel the wreckage of the blade as it opened me up from throat to navel, a hurried and merciless cut indifferent to the humanity of its subject. Every organ exposed, I was being wheeled out into courtrooms to bear muted witness to a rough, live autopsy of my every action and intention, and watching my vitals drop as I was committed to science.

———

On September 14, X filed to transfer jurisdiction. Once again, her request was denied, though not without more travel and expense on my part.

By the time we got to the matter at hand it was October 27, 2010. I had gotten the notice on August 2: "MUST complete the enclosed purple Intake form / MUST arrive 15 minutes prior to your appointment / Metered street parking, quarters only." Got it.

I was back in that drab public servant office of the mediator that marked the beginning of 2007 for me.

I advocated for the terms of the Global Agreement; the mediator questioned X; X retreated to silence.

"As you know, X has been picking the children up at 8:30 a.m. on Sunday mornings when I have them in order to, supposedly, go to church. However, I have learned from the children that it has been something like a year since they have been to church because 'Mom' doesn't like it. This is not right." I focused on anything I could win.

I remember the mediator confirming with X that church was no longer happening and saying, "Okay. Ms. Darné, what time would you like to send the children back on Sundays?"

Well, I wouldn't want them to be stressed for school. They need time to adjust. "3:00 p.m."

"Michelle shall provide the children's physical care for two consecutive weekends each month, from 5:00 p.m. on Thursday to 3:00 p.m. Sunday each weekend" found its way into the mediator's recommendations to the court. It is the only documentation from this session, however, as no transcript was produced.

We would share our children, like clothes, across a select number of holidays. Odd years. Even years. That is the low I had been taken to.

"Each parent may take up to two non-consecutive weeks of summer vacation with the children each year," the mediator wrote in her recommendations. For me, that would not provide extra time but rather disrupt my schedule, as X always scheduled her vacation over my regular parenting time.

We were not to engage in conflict in front of the children, discuss court, or allow others to disparage the other parent in any way.

The mediator's notes from November 1, 2010, would read:

"Michelle is requesting a custodial timeshare of one full week each month. Michelle proposed seven consecutive days but would be willing to have two long weekends instead. Michelle says the current schedule only allows her one and a half days with the girls every month, which is not enough. Michelle says she attained residence in Colorado for the sole purpose of having more custodial time with the children. Michelle says the children have repeatedly expressed a desire to spend more time with her.

"X is requesting to maintain the current schedule, although she agreed to extend Michelle's monthly weekend to Sunday 3:00 p.m. (instead of Sunday 8:30 a.m.). X says the children already struggle with the current schedule and often do not want to spend a weekend with Michelle. X says it would be difficult to make them see Michelle for a full week, or for two consecutive week-ends. X says Michelle has not honored the custodial time she has already been given, so should not be granted any additional time."

X says.

"The remaining areas of dispute," the mediator noted, were "whether there should be a change of venue (to Colorado) . . . Among other reasons for this request, X says that children's voices are heard in the state of Colorado and she would like the girls to be given the opportunity to voice their opinions regarding custody arrangements directly to the court, prior to making any changes."

A question posed by one of our judges resounded in my memory, addressing X on precisely this matter: "As a mother, do you really think it is a good thing for your children to take the stand at this early age?"

"Consequently," the mediator concluded in her statement, "the attached Memorandum of Understanding and all recommendations in this Status Report are pending the outcome of [*yet another costly, superfluous, manipulative*] request for a change of venue."

"Unless there are compelling reasons indicating otherwise," the mediator continued in her report, "it would be in the best interest of the children, at age seven, to have regular and consistent contact with both parents, regardless of their stated preferences. In this case, there do not seem to be valid reasons why Michelle's parenting time should be restricted."

I wanted to live in those words, to lie down in their shade and rest.

"If she is willing to commit to being available in Colorado on a regular and consistent basis, then the children would benefit from having both parents involved in their activities and routine."

These words were, to me, like the essence of truth itself.

"However, spending seven consecutive days away from X may be difficult for them. Therefore, it is recommended the children be with Michelle two consecutive weekends each month. The court should help parents determine if the second and third weekends are preferable, or the third and fourth weekends of each month."

I was not sure how the outlined rationale justified the ultimate restriction of my time with the children to only six days per month. However, I felt grateful to pick up three days with my daughters and to hold a piece of paper that acknowledged my value to them. Is that how systemic torment ensures submission? Is this how it wears an individual so thin that she relinquishes her sense of justice? Until she gratefully welcomes mere crumbs of her rights?

CHAPTER 10:
ROUND AND ROUND

RESILIENCE: the power or ability to return to the original form, position, etc., after being bent, compressed, or stretched; elasticity. Ability to recover readily from illness, depression, adversity, or the like; buoyancy.

Within weeks there was another 2:00 p.m. hearing—indistinguishable and thoroughly unnecessary from my perspective, but somehow vitally important—in California family court. This time, though, X's attorney slipped CPS (Child Protection Services) into a sentence. The next thing I knew, it sounded like she was suggesting I had called CPS on my ex-wife's household.

"Wait, wait a minute!" I remember interjecting, standing up in shock. "I have no idea what you are talking about. Why would CPS be getting involved? What is happening there?"

"It looks like Ms. Darné knows nothing about this situation," the judge, in essence, addressed X's attorney . Turning her head toward the court officer, she continued, "Please clear this court; this is a private matter."

I was a turbulent blend of worried paralysis and explosives while everybody extraneous cleared out. What the hell was happening to the children that was again bad enough for the judge to clear the jam-packed court?

Before I left, I learned that somebody had anonymously reported my ex-wife's household to CPS. Meticulous and lengthy proceedings had ensued, but there was deemed to be no case—just a misunderstanding. It was as good as over. And that was the inadequate extent of what I was entitled to know.

———

Later that night, while I sat, stunned by my new awareness, in my parents' kitchen, Juliette called my mobile.

"Mama!" She sounded furious with me. "Why did you call CPS on our family?"

"What are you talking about?!" Why the hell was my little daughter calling me out on this? Just how out of control was X, I wondered, and what in the world was going on in her household?

I told Juliette that I had done no such thing, but she would not believe it.

Dismayed and trying to make sense of everything, I made my way back to Colorado.

As soon as they opened for business the following morning, I was on the phone to CPS to find out what was happening to my children. I learned that somebody had reported my ex-wife's household to them, and that they had been involved for weeks investigating the claims.

"The reporter said that one of your daughters said she had been punished with a belt," they told me.

Alarms sounded in my head. One of the few things that X and I had agreed on was that we would not spank or belt our children—that violence only begets violence. For me, such agreements were set in stone and off the table for renegotiation by new partners. These decisions should be only between her and me, the two parents.

"However," the CPS worker continued, "your daughter will not confirm it. We have interviewed both children, been to their school twice, and spent some time in their home, and we believe it was a misunderstanding. The children are fine."

Thank god.

"A difference in parenting styles."

An alarmingly indifferent diagnosis.

"The case is nearly wrapped up now."

Wow. And you never even called me? Does anybody on this planet care that I am their other legal parent? The school had not called me either. I had been utterly left on the outside of an investigation into whether my children were being harmed. *How is that fuckin' possible?*

"Wait a minute, that's it? Case closed? That cannot be enough. These are my children, and I am only now finding out about all of this. There has got to be more that we can do to ensure, absolutely for certain, that they are safe."

The woman called me back the next day.

"Michelle, what we recommend is a mediated meeting before we close out this case. Am I right that another adult is living in your household?"

Yes; a girlfriend had moved in while she was getting her life sorted out.

"Both of you need to attend." She gave us a time and date.

———

We had been waiting in the lobby for forty-five minutes when the mediator came out.

"Ms. Darné, I am very sorry but they are not attending today. We have tried to contact them but have not been able to reach them."

The meeting was rescheduled, and I rearranged my flights to accommodate it. Same lobby, more waiting.

"Ms. Darné, you wouldn't believe it, but again they have not shown. I am so sorry you had to change your schedule to be here again, for nothing."

So was I.

"We cannot make this meeting mandatory, so there is nothing we can do."

Again, it was rescheduled.

—————

On December 16, 2010, after exhausting hesitation despite ardent advice from my attorney, I had filed against X to address my child support.

"I believe that all of Respondent's actions have been done in bad faith," states my plea. "First, by unilaterally backing out of our Global Agreement, then by unilaterally reducing my visitation time back to the original 11.66%, and then by filing the Motion for Change of Venue as a tactic meant to avoid having my Motion heard by the California court." I resented having to spell out the obvious, because it sounded unbelievable.

"The result," my plea continued, "is that my time with the children has been severely reduced and Respondent is enforcing a prior child support order for $1,250 per month against me." She was determined to have it all: to negate me and to have me pay for it. "I am now getting child support bills from the state of California AND the state of Colorado. At this point, I don't know what I should be paying and/or who I am supposed to pay it to." The child support caseworkers of two states were still hunting me with vigor. As if I was being punished for doing things by the book. As if I had been voted accountable for the actions of thousands of fathers who didn't pay and could not even be found. "Per Judge Mill's instructions at the last hearing,

I have made SEVERAL attempts to discuss the problems with the child support orders with [X's attorney], however she has ignored my letter and numerous phone calls / See Exhibit 'G.'"

Even framed crooks didn't deserve a callback, I suppose.

I asked the court "to reevaluate this situation so that I can be FAIRLY assessed the PROPER amount of child support and be fairly credited for the payments I have already made / [and] to IMPUTE FULL-TIME INCOME to Respondent." My financial responsibility had continued, nearly five years after our divorce, to reflect that X was a stay-at-home mom rather than a highly qualified designer with school-aged children.

The court order instigated the habitual flurry of court appearances. And elicited unprecedented fury from my ex-wife.

———

It was third-time-lucky for the meeting rearranged by the Colorado CPS. I do not remember what I had to miss, what work I forsook, in order to be in that confined space with X, Norma, my girlfriend at the time, a mediator, a whiteboard, and optimistically simplistic posters about domestic issues.

"It is my understanding," I said, "that the children are going to therapy; they told me so themselves. When I found out, I requested information on this from X, but she hasn't supplied it. This is what I am talking about. By law, she is supposed to keep me in the loop about our children where it pertains to healthcare, education—"

"You can talk to her," X interjected matter-of-factly, referring to the therapist.

"Okay! Give me her number." I wrote it down.

The meeting went on, but to my surprise, outside of me raising the issue of therapy, the session seemed to have nothing to do with the alleged punishment by belt and everything to do with me.

"Ms. Darné, we have been told that a lot of yelling and screaming goes on in your household," the mediator said. "Is that true?"

Wow. Am I under investigation here? It was as if at some point since my phone conversation with CPS, the workshop had been reframed around me as the underlying issue, and all parties had been notified . . . except me. I was further questioned on obstructing the children's right to call home when they were with me.

I had gotten used to seeing X icy cold, but now I wondered whether I had come face-to-face with the force that had stopped her heart. Norma was leaning back in her chair, arms folded, defiance and animosity contained between cowboy boots and a cowboy hat.

"Norma, are you planning to participate? We have not heard anything from you yet."

"I. Hate. Michelle."

All sound got expunged from the room. Everybody just looked at Norma.

Why the fuck would you say that? You have never spoken to me. You don't know me. I have never done anything to hurt you.

The mediator broke the silence. "Ms. Darné, how does that make you feel?"

"There is no love lost there," I responded calmly. "Her feelings toward me, or lack thereof, have nothing to do with the issue at hand."

The workshop went on, outputs transcribed on the wall.

After several inferences from X's corner that I had called CPS, I exclaimed, "Can somebody please tell these people that I was *not* the one who placed that phone call?" But they couldn't; it was an anonymous report.

"There is something I would like to say about that," I interjected when the topic of the transition the children experienced when they went from one household to the other came up. I vowed to have something good come out of this bogus experience. "I see the children change, literally, as they walk from my car to their door. They kiss me good-bye, leave the Jeep, and morph—their postures, their energy, changing completely. This cannot be good for them."

"Do you have any suggestions for how this can be made easier for the girls?" The mediator was attentive.

"Yes, I do. I think that we should acknowledge each other around the kids. Say hello. For their sake."

My recommendation didn't make it onto the board. A whole number of other points, however, did:

Juliette and Alyssa call Mom and Mommy at any time as often as they need or want.

Juliette and Alyssa can call a "time out" and take a break whenever they feel uncomfortable, unsafe, or upset.

All members of the family will use calm . . . indoor voices when they are having important conversations or upset.

Michelle will make phone available to the girls when they request one. [In case the first bullet didn't clearly enough stipulate that our children's relationship with Mommy and Mom wasn't sacredly protected during my sixty-three monthly hours with the girls. But not the other way around.]

No members of the family can talk to the girls about the DHS case unless they bring it up to them.

No members of family will threaten to or spank Juliette or Alyssa at any time.

All parents in the family will use "time outs" as punishment for Juliette and Alyssa when they are misbehaving. Then, the girls will be asked what they did wrong and they will tell what they can do better next time.

All parents will not talk to Juliette and Alyssa about the court unless they specifically ask.

All parents will use extra chores as punishment for Juliette and Alyssa when they are misbehaving (as another potential).

I received this list of outcomes, dated December 20, 2010, and written out in studious block letters, already signed by X, Norma, and the children themselves. My girlfriend and I countersigned.

On that very December 20, I was in court in California, where Judge Scanlon adopted the Memorandum of Understanding from our second mediation in October. On that same day, I was issued another letter by the Department of Human Services of Larimer County, Colorado. Curt, it stated:

"Dear Ms. Darne, The Larimer County Department of Child Support Enforcement is enforcing the above identified child support case. As a requirement of our office, it is necessary for all future child support payments to be made to the following address . . . You will not be given credit for any child support payments made direct to the custodial parent . . . Attached, please find an updated arrears calculation." Signed: Patsy, Child Support Accounting Department.

———

That Christmas was hell.

The children insisted on unwrapping their gifts as soon as they got them; I barely got a smile or a hug. And they were outraged with me because they only got clothes. But they needed clothes. X would not allow them to bring any with them. It was a bitter-cold winter, but they wouldn't even have jackets on when they got into my Jeep. And I could not afford much more. As it was, my parents had chipped in.

I wished I could scream. How could children be so very cruel? Why could I not have one moment, one night, one Christmas when my face wasn't rubbed in how much I was failing them?

Come Christmas morning, the phone would not stop ringing. Similarly, they would not stop calling Mommy. Finally, I picked up.

"Please, X," I appealed to her, "I am in the middle of talking to the children about the reasons they are so upset, of trying to work it out with them. Let up."

But Mommy was in every moment of our day. The children demanded that I take them to her, without any explanation. Whenever any of us were upset, I made sure that we didn't run away from it. We always talked it through, they always bared their hearts, and we always found a way forward together. But not this time. They were simply furious with me for reasons beyond my understanding.

At some point, I gave up and called X. "Fine, you can come pick them up." Gluttonous victory hung up on defeat. My children didn't even want to be here. They didn't want to be with me. I had tried but failed to figure out what was wrong. Some parent. I was a stressor. An infecting splinter. Deserving of extraction from their Christmas Day.

Before I could blink, X was at my front door. Relaxed, reliable, comforting; robed in smiles, oohs, and aahs; whisking my happy-once-more children away.

———

I spent those holidays alone. In a big, empty house. On January 8, 2011, armed with our second inadequate parenting agreement, I e-mailed X confirming pickup and drop-off arrangements for the two weekends I would have with the children that month.

On January 10, X replied, "Neither we, nor you are permitted to lay in a particular weekend to the court order, because it's considered 'tampering.' Are you willing to mediate this out of court? . . . (please note: in light of the ongoing cps investigation, and what happened at your place Christmas day, I don't feel good about any of this.)"

Writing back that day, I recited the part of the mediator's report saying that I would "provide the children's physical care for two consecutive weekends each month," and said that I was "willing to do either the 2nd and 3rd weekend or the 3rd and 4th weekend—you choose, of course we can mediate this among ourselves and out of court." I added, "As for the ongoing investigation with CPS (again, I have nothing to do with this). And, 'in light of what happened at my house on Christmas Day' . . . I have no idea what you are referring to. However, I am open to discuss if you would like to discuss."

In another twenty minutes, X replied. "Provide me some documentation that has you agreeing to the 2nd and 3rd weekend, with your signature and date, so I can give it to [my attorney]." As usual, I was frustrated that nothing could be straightforward with X; we hadn't needed five e-mails, on top of everything else, to reach a resolution. I was glad she was providing a way forward; however, her e-mail didn't end there. "I truly fear for the kids' safety being in your care. No child should have to suffer that on Christmas day. I was nervous for them before . . . now this is scary." Another dig against my worn-down defenses.

Across several more e-mails that followed, we agreed where I would fax my agreement to the chosen weekends, which I did on January 14. But I did not get my allotted parenting time that month. I sent my letter via certified mail to X's attorney, who signed for it on January 31, 2011, but that did not make a difference. Judge Scanlon did not sign the order until February 16, 2011; it was February 17 when it got filed. I lost two months of parenting time, and I felt masterfully put in my place.

Around the same time, one of X's friends, Melanie, had called me because her parenting time (she had one daughter, only a year younger than my girls) fell on the same days as mine. She asked if all three children could play together.

Melanie was among the first people the children had met in their new Colorado life, and she was very engaged with the whole family. The girls were ecstatic when I told them about the play date; on X's time, they were spending a lot of time together and were very close.

I opened the door in my robe; Melanie required urging before she stepped inside. It was the first time we had interacted, and I could only imagine what she thought of me. However, she was the only one who had always taken my call when she happened to have the children during my daily scheduled call with them. X was hit or miss, and everybody else, including the babysitters, wouldn't even pick up, as if I were indeed deleted, despite the court order that stipulated my right to talk to the children every evening. So I appreciated her without ever having met her before.

After that evening, we agreed to get together more frequently when our parenting times coincided.

According to Melanie, she had confirmed with X that it was okay to reach out to me. However, after she did make contact, both X and her new partner appeared to change their minds. They came over to her house and delivered a book on sociopaths and their behavior. "That's what Michelle is like," they assured her. Melanie must not have reacted appropriately, because shortly after, this friend felt disowned, cut out of their lives after being quite embedded for years. I did not know any of this for about six months, until I made some reference to her frequent times in X's household and was corrected.

As we spent more time together, I was seeing just how Melanie was with my girls. They had spent countless days together, often on her farm and also on day trips, at fairs, and at various kid birthday parties. Herself probably unaware of just how patchy my knowledge of their lives was at that stage, as Melanie shared the photos and the heartfelt anecdotes from their childhoods, she was filling many gaps for me.

"Michelle," she said one evening, her voice unusually awkward and apologetic. "You may want to change your e-mail password."

"Why?" The suggestion came absolutely out of nowhere, and I couldn't see a single reason for it.

"I am just saying; may be a good idea."

I did not heed her advice, or grasp her reason for giving it. It wasn't until later that I learned that X had been breaking into my e-mails ever since we separated—for nearly three years at that point.

"Should you be doing this?" Melanie said she asked X one day.

"Why not?" X responded. "If she is an idiot enough not to change her passwords, that's on her."

I could not believe what I was hearing. First of all, where in the world do people find time to do this shit? My life resembled that of a hamster in a wheel, and that was just to keep up. Meanwhile, here was an individual actually dedicating her time to sifting through my inbox.

As I thought about it, I felt more and more disgusted by X's behavior. Never in my life had I felt an impulse to pry into people's private matters, and I could not fathom why anybody would. I hadn't even considered changing my passwords after our divorce—obviously a blind spot on my part. Now it made sense why she seemed to be apprised of my life way beyond the degree to which I was sharing it with her; now I understood why she appeared to know and scrutinize my schedule, and why she sometimes made sly comments about people and events I was involved with. All this shed new light on her claim from years ago that I could do nothing without her finding out.

Inside my head, my heart, and my workday, I recognized remnants, traces of my ravager. I had been violated—and more than anything else, I felt tricked by human nature, by the disgrace it was capable of. I could not believe I had been hoaxed by a person who had once chosen to marry me and now took a sick pleasure in parading me before others as a fool.

In addition to realizing that my ex-wife felt entitled to callously trespass on my life, over the course of a couple of weeks I also learned a great deal about the environment in the children's other home from my new eyewitness, Melanie.

"I've got to tell you," she shared on several occasions when she watched the girls run around the house, laughing, or when they were helping themselves to a snack in the kitchen, "they are so much more relaxed here at your house, like they can just be themselves." She told me that they were required to call Norma "Mom" and were reprimanded if they didn't. I recalled that indeed it was mere months after moving in with her that the children started referring to her that way. *How cruel,* I thought to myself. *Why force them when they were going through so much change, missing their other parent?* Assuming the relationship was nurturing, wouldn't they have gotten there on their own?

I learned that X had also had a hand in the countless sleepovers that had reduced my little time with the children. I had usually been left under the impression that the invites just happened to fall on my time, and that she would merely ask those hosts to contact me directly. I, of course, never wanted to disrupt the children's routine, so I always said yes.

I also learned that the children weren't allowed to come into X and Norma's bed, even if they were scared; it was off-limits. X had to sneak upstairs, into the attic repurposed for the children, if they were unwell or sad and she wanted to lie with them to soothe them.

However systemic or accidental those instances, what I was hearing about the way that our children were being treated in X's house made no sense to me. I was struggling to recognize my ex-wife in this behavior. She had always been warm and affectionate toward the girls; why had she adopted this militant approach?

Melanie also repeatedly mentioned how much, and with great fondness, X had apparently talked about the life she used to have—the people she had met, the exclusive experiences she had been part of. Of course, she never linked any of it to me, never suggested that this was the life she had had while we were married.

These stories seemed fantastical to me. Melanie appeared to be describing a woman that was vain, materialistic, and opportunistic, and the X I knew did not care about money, let alone access, and had hated the side of our life, and of me, that involved glamour. So I dismissed those stories as one perspective on a situation. Even having been pounded into the ground by X, I opted for denial—I hung on to what she had always said about herself and insisted on there being another explanation for her actions. Perhaps I wasn't ready to accept what was being made apparent because it would invalidate the little that remained intact about the truth of my life.

CHAPTER 11:

SUCKER PUNCH

AMBUSH: an act or instance of lying concealed so as to attack by surprise.

It was March 2011. My daughters' eighth birthday was approaching, and with it another assured misfortune: I would not be able to see them that day.

When X decided that my parenting time should fall on the second and third weeks of the month, I automatically conceded; we had a resolution, and I was going to see the children more. *The weekends won't really matter*, I thought, picking my battles. But it soon became apparent that this allocation made sure that both X's and Norma's birthdays fell on X's time, that I almost never had the children for my birthday, and never, not once, would we be together on theirs. By this point, it was five years and counting.

So, as per usual, I was planning a birthday party for the girls at the next available time, which on this year should have been the second weekend in April. First, however, I had to make it back to court for the next, hopefully final, hearing regarding my child support, which was set for April 5, 2011.

Shortly after I got back from the hearing, Melanie called.

"Hey, could I come by and talk to you?" She sounded anxious.

"Sure," I said. "Is everything okay?"

"Yeah, well . . . I just need to talk to you."

I finished unpacking and started dinner while I waited for her.

When she arrived, I sensed her discomfort and got her a cup of coffee before we sat down in the living room.

"Michelle, look," she started what felt like a confession rattling its way out. "Here are some things I feel like I need to share. I can't keep it inside any longer. But I don't know how to put them."

"It's okay, you can talk to me," I assured her, still oblivious to what was bothering her so much.

"Remember this past Christmas, when I came with X to pick the girls up on Christmas Day?"

"Of course. How can I forget?"

"Well, it was all planned to happen that way." Melanie explained that plans had been made to go to somewhere on Christmas Day, during my holiday with the children, and the girls knew all about these irresistible, fun-filled plans. I had been set up to stand, oblivious, between the children and that fun; the odds had been mercilessly stacked against me.

"And that woman who was seeing the kids for 'counseling' who would never speak with you; remember her?" Melanie continued.

"Of course." After I got her number at that CPS workshop, I had called a couple of times. When I finally got her on the phone, all she said was, 'I cannot discuss this right now,' and explained that she had something else starting at that time. So we scheduled a time to talk, but she didn't show up for it. She didn't return my subsequent calls, either.

"She is a very close friend of Norma's," Melanie continued, emboldened by the relief of these confessions.

She was never going to talk to me, I realized, disheartened. I had thought I could establish contact with a professional who was treating my children, and instead I stumbled into enemy territory and had been made into a laughingstock.

"There is something else . . ."

I was still caught up in my dismay at how much sense Melanie had just made of my flabbergasting Christmas experience, but she was waiting for me to make room for another revelation.

"It is about the girls." Melanie acted sheepish, like a dog that knows it has misbehaved, as she told me that one of my girls had been forced to stay in the bathroom until she pulled out her own loose tooth. As I listened, I could picture my little girl clearly: terrified but defiant, sobbing in distress, mad at the stubborn tooth, and confined to a tiled cell where she fell asleep on the floor, bloodied by her own dauntless efforts.

What I was hearing was crushing a reality I had long held dear despite X's attacks on me: a belief that they were always safe in her care. Melanie's eyewitness accounts would have been disturbing in any case, but they were especially petrifying and bewildering to me given that the girls were not yet even eight years old. I felt myself filling up with anger, like a balloon. And the balloon burst when Melanie admitted to having seen belt marks on Juliette and said that Juliette later shared with Melanie's friend about being hit with a belt.

So the CPS experience wasn't the nuisance it was made out to be!? The information about the belt had been right there in front of me for nearly five months, but I had sat on my hands. What kind of system of child protection was this? It had failed my children even more than it had failed me when they didn't even consider informing me about the allegations they were investigating.

I could have done something! What kind of mother am I if I let them trick me into dismissing what I heard? And what kind of mother DOES THAT?

My fragile world was coming undone, dishing up memories, moments, and phrases now reframed with new significance.

"Mom said that you made that agreement with Mommy about not hitting us." Alyssa's statement, uttered casually in her sweet, groggy voice, pierced the cacophony of my thoughts. "She said it had nothing to do with her or with our household."

How could I do my job as a mother, how could I foresee—and prevent—the worst that could happen to my girls, if cornerstone agreements were nothing but shifting sand?

I don't remember when Melanie left. Despair was raging within the walls of my kind house. The erratic realizations that followed Melanie's visit had cast me to the floor; grief and guilt were bouncing off the walls and stabbing me senseless as I wailed into the universe.

What kind of mother am I if I can't keep my children safe?

The sun traversed the sky a couple of times before I emerged from the confines of my mind, noticed my surroundings, and regained a sense of time. My children were coming home that week.

I don't remember why, but I wouldn't be picking them up on Thursday, as I usually did, but rather on Saturday, April 9. And I would only be picking up Juliette, as Alyssa was at a sleepover or some such event. I drove pensively, focusing on my breathing. I needed to stay calm, to subdue the rage seething within me.

Upon pulling up, I got out of the car just as Juliette got in. X had seen her off and was standing outside. I went up to her and handed her the gift bag to give to Alyssa for the birthday party happening that afternoon. Then I said, "I don't know what's going on here, but tell your girlfriend to keep her f***ing hands off our kids."

I walked back to the car and got in. X started pursuing me, angry and screaming.

"Get out of the car!" she yelled at our little, horrified kid that had buckled herself into the backseat. "Now!"

"It's okay, it's okay; go on into the house," I said as reassuringly as I could.

Juliette bolted.

X screamed for a neighbor who never came out and yelled that she was calling the cops.

I decided to cancel the birthday party and stay put, but after I had been outside X's house for twenty minutes and the cops had still not shown up, I left to go home.

I drove home. By the time I arrived, I had a voice message on my phone, left while my phone had no reception through the mountains.

The call was from a police officer who introduced himself, stated that his call was regarding the incident at X's house, and asked me to please call him back.

I immediately did, and when he answered, I told him exactly what I had said to X, f-word and all. I was still shocked, feeling like essential power had been stolen from me by my ex-wife.

"What kind of mother am I if I cannot protect my children, and who else do I have to talk to besides her?" I demanded. "What mother wouldn't be enraged? Wouldn't say what I said, if not worse?"

"She said you grabbed her."

I did not. Later, even our daughter who witnessed the scene confirmed that I had not grabbed or otherwise touched or hit X.

"There was no crime committed," the officer concluded before ending our phone call.

Despite my continued attempts to pick up the children during that parenting time, I got no response; I didn't even get to speak to the children to confirm that they were okay. My attorney advised that even though X had not honored my parenting time, quite a few steps would be involved in doing anything about that, and it might not be worth the fight.

The next parenting time came around—Thursday, April 14—and I arrived for "curbside pickup." Neither X nor the children appeared to be there, but a man I had never seen before was standing outside and looking in my direction.

He approached the car. "Are you Michelle Darné?"

"Yes," I said, confused.

He was extending a half-an-inch-thick package to me. Just as I reached to receive it, he pronounced, "You have been served."

The man fell out of my field of vision; I fixated on the papers. At the top of the packet was X's Petition for Allocation of Parental Responsibilities. Despite the rulings of the California Court, X had filed against me in Colorado to determine custody, child support, and related matters. This suit was throwing the meager rights I had won back up in the air.

I continued flipping through the pages of associated Notices of Initial Status Conference, Case Management Order, and the like. I paused on the affidavit X had included regarding the children. Norma was listed first on the list of "all persons the children have lived with within the last five years." Under Relationship to Child, X had stated, "Parental role in our house; they call her Mom. I was listed number four: "Parenting occasionally 2007 to present." Our children had been born in 2003. But right above her signature, the affidavit read, "I swear or affirm under penalty of perjury that information contained in this Affidavit Regarding Children is true and correct."

I knew I had pissed her off by challenging our financial arrangement. However, with this suit she took the retaliation I had grown to expect to a whole new level. How the hell was I supposed to fight this one?

Then, my thoughts and my fingers froze. Disoriented, I just stared. A temporary restraining order. Seeing those words on the page, all wind abandoned my sails, leaving them flapping, limp, empty.

"It is ordered that you, the Restrained Person, shall have no contact of any kind with the Protected Persons." The list included X as well as both our daughters. "NO EXCEPTIONS." My ex-wife had finally stumbled upon a particularly cunning method for cutting me out of my daughters' lives. Despair infiltrated me like smoke, oozing through the cracks in my resolve, discounting the barriers of rational thought, and suffocating my faith.

There was a victoriously empty box next to "Restrained Person is granted Parenting Time with the minor children." X was peddling a unique blend of helplessness and posturing, and it was growing more potent.

She had filed all this right after our last encounter. The hearing was scheduled for 10:00 a.m. on April 25, 2011.

Through my haze, my mind somehow registered the grave consequences of what had just occurred. I called my attorney in California. She was off work—it was the weekend—but she immediately helped me find local representation. The clock was ticking for me to file a contrary motion and to show up in court with an attorney.

In keeping with X's approach over the past few years, the Restraining Order Argument (some sixteen pages of it) was compelling, full of incidents that had indeed occurred, just not the way they were described. They had been spliced, edited, positioned, and distorted just enough to trigger fury—and crucify me.

What must have sealed the deal with the court was this: "The Protected Person has requested that the address be omitted from the written order of the court." Did she take exquisite pleasure in these theatrics? Who was she trying to fool? I had been picking the children up at her house for years, and her address was all over the dozen other motions, petitions, and orders floating within the abyss of family court.

What followed next was a two-hour briefing meeting that my new attorneys graciously scheduled for that Saturday morning, with a 7:00 a.m. start time. Michael was standing outside as I pulled into the parking lot—gray-haired, distinguished, and ready to sweep up the wreck that was me out of the car.

If we lost, I would not see my children for four years. I hadn't slept, eaten, or stopped crying since my face-off with X. Worse, I hadn't seen or spoken to the girls. My resolve was recoiling, curling up like a leaf by the fire, replaced by encroaching dread.

Even though I had fought injustice, and X, circumstances, and even the darn Colorado snow, for years leading up to this moment, the restraining order had floored me. Perhaps it was because I felt—or wanted to feel—that the battle was over and I could now just build my life with the children, all six days per month of it. Perhaps it was because I was still depleted from everything I had already gone through. Or perhaps it was because it was the most unfounded, manipulative ploy X had pulled—and it had a very good chance of getting by our legal system. When the alleged victim is a seemingly affable, helpless biological mommy and the alleged aggressor is a scrappy, straight-shooting brown chick that kisses no ass and deploys f-words, the outcome seems almost predetermined.

A restraining order is that rare legal tool that makes no presumption of innocence until proven guilty. This means that the accused must prove innocence or the restraining order reins in its devastating might. Fear was taking root in my soul, edging out the light.

I remember my attorney's kind eyes as he was waiting in the parking lot to help me. He walked me into his office, where for two hellish hours I relived my entire story. Through tea and my tears, we prepared my defense for a crime I hadn't committed.

———

An old plank dock extends out into the water. It is shaped like an inverted L. There is water on both sides, and I marvel at the outlines of mountains cupping the lake. There is no doubt that the dock could tell many a story; it looks like it has been here for decades, and it is worn and rickety. The light is devoid of time, the kind of light that could marshal a morning or a dusk. The air is dark, foggy, thick.

I can feel my children, smell them, hear them on the cellular level.

And there they are! In the distance, running along the dock toward me. Yelling, "Mama! Mama! Mama!" they make the turn onto the straightaway toward me. Their faces come into greater focus. They look so grown-up! Thirteen or fourteen, they are already much taller than me; how time flies. I lean forward, bending my knees a little, ready for them to ram into me. But they are not getting closer; they are running ever faster and yet vanishing farther into the distance. I take a step, stretch my arms out further, fight to keep them in focus, but they are fading. The dock has morphed into a reverse conveyor belt that is cruelly outpacing them. I can feel their growing angst through the heavy air.

I woke from this dream sobbing, time after time, for weeks, my body drenched in sweat as if tasered by this recurring nightmare.

On one night in particular the deep night sky surrounded me, looking in through the windows all around. The stars, usually so isolated and cold, seemed in accord, flickering responsively; tonight, it was me who was solitary. My heart, shattered into a million pieces; the sky, content in its immensity. Itself invincible, it attended to me as I wept, hoping to convey to me some of its timeless assuredness. "But I am not like you," I moaned. "I am not self-contained, I am not sovereign . . ."

But it didn't budge. Palpable, present, it stood watch over me as I was attacked by doubts, blindsided by rational explanations more unsettling than the events they made sense of. I wrestled with the legion of simultaneous, indignant thoughts that ambushed my disoriented mind as it struggled to grasp on to the new day. Thoughts that started, and ended, with a *why?* that was left wanting.

If any of what is happening is X's doing, why would she do it? I was asking myself. Since all this affected our children and not just me, why would she let it? Why would she let them believe what wasn't so? Could she possibly be so cruel as to accept the harm to them as the cost of getting back at me?

And then my mind wandered to the worst-case scenario, and I saw my life without any contact with my daughters, being forced to love them from afar. I felt a void, an emptiness, a helpless futility that was like a tsunami to the evening tide of all my prior suffering.

My body ached; raw fear rendered each cell tender, defenseless. Sobs escaped my throat, sharp like razors. I wished to dissolve into the earth; I almost felt its magnetic power tingling in my fingers, pulling me closer. Perhaps I could die.

"Stand up!" My mother's voice burst into me, harsh and dissonant, though she was hundreds of miles away. "You're strong! You never give up; you have been through tough times before."

But not like this, Mom.

"Stop it! You are not a quitter!"

Robed in the remnants of my frightening sleep, fear lingering in every thought, I dragged myself out of bed and made my way past my daughters' empty bedroom and down the stairs. I poured myself a cup of coffee, and my day began.

By this point I was embroiled in four distinct court battles with X. In California, I was just wrapping up the case to reconsider child support in one court and was dealing with the case X had filed (again) to move jurisdiction in another court; the hearing for that one was scheduled for April 27. In Colorado, she had filed a brand-new case to assess my custody, and now there was the restraining order, to be heard on April 25.

Naturally, I barely remember anything from that April besides court; besides jetting back and forth between Colorado and California; besides wondering how the girls were. There were thousands of dollars in legal fees that maxed out my emergency credit card. There were relentless nightmares, moments of realization that I may not see my children again, the agony of helplessness in keeping them safe, the debilitating awakening to the fact that any parenting decisions X and I had made together now had no hold.

Under all this, an old, throbbing wound had been reopened: the law was on X's side, no matter how little regard she had for it. It was to X's house that CPS had been summoned, yet the law deemed that I, the "(Restrained Person) constitute[ed] a credible threat" and that "an imminent danger exist[ed] to the life and health of the Protected Persons named in this action."

No matter the truth or the impact her schemes had on our children, my ex-wife wielded hypnotizing power over the system. It seemed she was invincible, immune to the consequences of her wrongdoings.

The days seemed never to end. I couldn't eat or sleep, so I painted my house, coat after coat—always a cathartic experience for me, and now the only thing I could actually do. As well as the only feeling I could access of wiping the slate clean, of restoring the tarnished to effervescence.

———

On April 13, after discussing the move with me at length, my California lawyer, Rebecca, filed for "Substitution of Attorney."

"Even your attorney does not want to be with you!" X told me after she was notified.

"How dare you!" I wanted to say, but I didn't. It was none of her business. My attorney's choice had nothing to do with me, and she had made sure to leave me in good hands with Gail and Michael. I didn't say a word.

I barely remember how my attorneys and I managed to

prepare a response to my ex-wife's petition to allocate parental responsibilities in Colorado.

"The issues of parentage, parenting time, and child support have already been addressed by the Superior Court of California," our argument read. "Petitioner should not be allowed to file a new Petition for Allocation of Parental Responsibilities in Colorado simply because she disagrees with the decisions of the Contra Costa Court."

We lodged this response on April 24, 2011, the day before I had my only opportunity to prove my innocence in the allegations of the Temporary Restraining Order.

There was another routine hearing scheduled in California the next day. I had been in my attorney's office in California when she was losing patience with the clerks at the court about this one.

"Listen to what I am saying!" she demanded. "I realize that Ms. Darné is supposed to attend every court hearing in person. However, she has another hearing in Colorado just a day earlier, and she simply cannot be in two places at the same time. I need you to allow a court call this time."

She got it for me.

———

The plane touched down. I had only a small window of time before the call, so I had mapped out my entire route to the specific payphone in the baggage claim area of Denver International Airport where it was relatively quiet.

When it came time to disembark, the crew kept shuffling around the door, but it wasn't opening. Then the announcement was made: the airplane door wasn't engaging, but they would do everything they could to get us out as soon as possible. *Stupid, careless fuckin' door, how dare you do this to me.* My legs were shaking, and I was looking at my phone every few seconds, desperate for time to stop, for them to fix whatever the issue was and get me the heck off this plane.

"Are you okay?" I must have been freaking out the lady next to me.

"I have to make a call; I will be late for a call."

"Well." She looked at the phone in my hand. "Can't you just make that call from here?"

"No, you don't understand!" She did not deserve my anger, but it was right there, crawling under my skin. "I have a court call! They do not permit calls from mobile phones. I have to get off this flight."

When they finally opened the door, I, who usually lets everybody pass so that I walk in peace, pushed people out of my way and started running, sprinting across the oversized terminal to the train, invoking all the power of my mind to make my body go faster, bounding up one escalator and down another, and then dialing the number with shaking fingers before my feet even fully arrived at the pay phone.

"Oh, there you are, Ms. Darné. We have been waiting for you. We gave you a couple more minutes before we marked you as a no-show."

Bent over the booth, catching my breath, I took the caustic jab.

As soon as the hearing was over, I made a beeline to the car rental and drove home.

———

The following morning, I was waiting in the lobby with my attorney for our scheduled 9:00 a.m. court appearance. I was now a mere ghost of myself, immensely short on sleep, faith, and dignity.

X walked in with her attorney, gave me a stare that felt like a raid, and took a seat on the other side of the lobby. We had subpoenaed the police officer that had handled the incident, and I saw him going through security. We knew that he would testify that "there was no crime committed" and that I had had a legal right to say what I said.

I, the so-called criminal, sat anticipating the hearing when X's attorney made his way across the lobby to us.

"May I speak to you in private?" he addressed my attorney, who nodded and got up. They walked off, out of my sight, while I numbly waited. I knew I might be served another curveball upon their return, but I no longer had it in me to even get anxious.

My attorney returned after about ten minutes, his step motivated.

"Look, I have some good news," he told me. "X has decided to drop the suit as long as you two have no further communication besides text and e-mail."

"Do we not get to see the magistrate? Do I not get a chance to tell her what really happened?" I could not believe I was being asked to throw in the towel, to concede. I wasn't even prepared to react to the proposal he was articulating. It didn't feel like victory; it felt worse than defeat, because it wouldn't allow me to clear my name.

"This is the best way for this to go away," my attorney said.

The resulting Stipulated Order Regarding dismissal of Temporary Protection Order and Entry of No Contact Order stated that "the temporary civil protection order issued on April 11, 2011, [was] vacated." It also stated, across two separate stipulations, that neither of us was to approach the other, and that we must "remain at least three yards away" from each other at all times.

This pseudo act of concession from X was not a vindication; it felt like a life sentence. And I have continued to feel like she has sought out opportunities to enforce it ever since. She is the judge, the jury, and the prosecutor, invincible before the law.

Time and time again, X has used her dropping those charges to imply that she was gracious even though I was a criminal. One third party even received an unsolicited e-mail from X informing them that if not for her graciousness, I would have lost my rights and access to the children due to my criminal and reckless character.

According to an article in the journal *Family Court Review*, 63 percent of all restraining orders are granted on the word of the plaintiffs alone.[4] The authors write that "allegations of abuse are now used for tactical advantage in divorce and child custody." Once again, I was a mere unfortunate statistic.

How was it okay for one human being to repeatedly undermine another's relationship with her children? To withhold court-ordered access? To threaten further alienation if one should resort to the courts? To bleed her financially and not skip a beat? How do the judges issue rulings that are meant to be "in the best interests of minor children" and yet eviscerate one of their parents? How do the clerks write it all up? How, tell me, is such behavior against a parent acceptable under the law?

———

I went straight to the airport from the courthouse. With barely twenty-four hours logged in Colorado, I boarded a flight back to California for the next day's hearing, where X's petition to "transfer the custody portion of the action to Colorado" would be considered.

This time, I conceded.

"Unless the case is transferred to Colorado, you have no protection there when X does not give you the kids or pulls something like the restraining order," my attorneys told me. "From California, it takes us months to get you to see the judge. It is time, Michelle."

The next status conference on the suit X had filed against me in Colorado was on May 4, 2011. However, the judge stated that the California orders held and that she had no jurisdiction

---

4. Johnston, J. R., S. Lee, N.W. Olesen, and M.G. Walters (2005). "Allegations and Substantiations of Abuse in Custody-disputing Families." *Family Court Review* 43: 283–294.

to rule on any of this unless the case was moved to Colorado. She dismissed the case.

Even after both the Colorado and the California courts issued their rulings, X wouldn't let me see the children. Finally, my attorney had to write a letter to hers. Dated May 13, 2011, it read:

> "It has come to my attention that Ms. Darné was not able to exercise parenting time this weekend. According to the Stipulated Order signed by Magistrate Berenato on May 10, 2011, the current California parenting time orders are in effect . . . Ms. Darné has parenting time two consecutive weekends each month . . . Since these orders came into effect on February 16, 2011, Ms. Darné has been denied the second weekend of parenting time each month . . . Ms. Darné makes arrangements to travel to Colorado to spend parenting time with Alyssa and Juliette, and your client has repeatedly denied her the opportunity to spend time with their daughters."

————

By the time I finally saw my children, it was summer. I was depleted; my work had gone neglected and required urgent interventions; I had barely eaten in weeks; and the girls were livid with me.

Whenever they spoke, it seemed, they would say something like, "Why would you do this to Mommy?" or "How could you do this to our family?" I could only suspect they were referring to the CPS investigation of their other house, or to the many court hearings of the past months, but I would not ask them to clarify for fear of engaging them deeper in issues that should not be on their minds in the first place.

What's more, I knew I had no answers that could satisfy their rage while protecting their childhood. I was still grappling with the court system's sense of reality, given that it had imposed greater constraints on me while admitting there were no grounds for X's charge. The bitterly ironic closing line of the order was replaying in my mind: "This Stipulated Order is in the best interest of the minor children, Juliette and Alyssa."

It would be difficult not to disparage X had I answered any of the girls' questions. It was obvious that they needed to believe she was infallible. I took this to be a primal instinct upon which their very survival depended. To protect their innocence, I had to not only be her audience but her coconspirator. What hurt the most was that in their eyes, in standing up for their safety, I had become the one they could no longer trust.

Children see things in black and white. To them this was Snow White versus the Evil Queen—and I was not going to be cast as Snow White. The life to which we had been sentenced was chipping away at the shards of space my children could leave for me in their hearts.

Even harder than accepting that my children saw me as a betrayer, and waiving any right to defend myself to them, was watching the best in our daughters, all that which made them children, manipulated. Their innocence, their purity, their translucent need for safety, their timeless certainty about how the world worked, their unscathed boldness, their illiteracy in shame, and their faith in X's infallibility had all been itemized and deployed by X in the battle for vindication.

———

After I dropped the children off one Sunday after an arduous three and a half days, I was driving back through town when I got pulled over.

"Driver's license and insurance, please," the officer said.

"Excuse me, did I do something wrong?" Spent, my mind couldn't register what I could have possibly done.

"Driving above the speed limit."

"Really? Isn't it forty miles per hour through here?"

"Yes."

"And how fast was I going?"

"Forty-two."

I could not believe what I was hearing, but he continued before I could say anything.

"And we have a bigger problem, Ms. *Darn*."

"It is *Darné*," I said—and there I went and pissed him right off. By this stage I was standing outside my Jeep.

"Your driver's license has been suspended."

Through those months, I had again fallen behind on child support. My California caseworkers were checking in but remained understanding and respectful. That had never been the style of the Colorado child support system, however, which had sent me a letter threatening to suspend my driver's license (not issued by the state of Colorado, mind you), all because of that redundant, ludicrous case my ex-wife had opened there.

"Are you serious?" I demanded.

"Get back! FOUR FEET BACK!" I must have raised my voice, because the officer was shouting as if I were about to attack him. "I have the right to take you into custody; I can take you to jail."

"What?!" I could not let this twenty-something rookie out to prove his worth take me to jail. "Can you just call my attorney?"

He didn't want to budge, but his partner, who had witnessed the entire first act, looked at him, and he obliged. I dialed Gail, praying that she would pick up on a Sunday afternoon.

Thankfully, she did, and she proceeded to talk sense into the overzealous cop.

"Here is your ticket," he said. "You cannot drive. You have to leave the Jeep here."

"Officer . . . can you please just follow me up to the house, I'll put the Jeep in the garage—"

His resolute head shaking interrupted me. "Call a cab."

I will not scream, I told myself. *I will not LOSE IT!* I had no cash on me; in fact, thanks to the last couple of senseless months, I had no money at all.

After feeling forced to secure a friggin' permission to do so, I moved the Jeep around the corner, where it would not get towed, and the officers left. Then I called Melanie, who, thankfully, was able to come get me. I waited for her on the sidewalk, devastated, exhausted from having my pleas for justice ignored, and battered by having to tame my fury so as to avoid provoking a system that seemed to care only for making a trophy of me.

While I waited for Melanie for what turned out to be three quarters of an hour, the officers drove past me several times. In their eyes I was but a fugitive criminal, ready but unable, on their vigilant watch, to run from the law.

———

At some point during that summer, Melanie asked to come over with a friend of hers.

"I have to tell you something," the friend started. "I can no longer watch you be punished for calling CPS." She was visibly burdened by what had compelled her to come over. "I called them after Melanie saw those belt marks and Juliette told me what had been happening." She was a juvenile officer and was obligated to report the incident, but she felt terrible for how it had backfired on me.

So I hadn't been crazy that whole time. I felt vindicated. This brave woman was among only a handful of people, over the course of now a decade, who had taken a stand for the girls and against a broken and biased legal system. I was grateful to her, especially since I have not heard of any further instances.

I never told the children who reported to CPS, or why; my job as a parent wasn't to make them like me, especially if it could only be achieved by throwing another person in their life under the bus. My job was to shield them from the parts of the world they could not understand at their age, and to show up for them. To love them unconditionally, even when it scorched me like acid. No matter what.

It took more time before I saw them two weekends a month more often than not. And during the little time we had together, for months, no matter what I said, my little daughters continued to crucify me for calling CPS on their family. But their anger was now easier to take—so, for their sake, I continued to pay the price for another's crime against them.

Perhaps this book will put me in that position again, but so be it if it saves even one person from experiencing what happened to me. By doing what I must, by doing all that I can so that my story can be committed to the pages of history, and so that the girls can grow up in a more just society, I may again have to pay the price for everything, convicted for being wronged.

EPILOGUE

INSIGHT: an understanding of relationships that sheds light on or helps solve a problem.

It has been over six years since my last court appearance. I wish it were because there has been no need—because our two households have reached an amicable arrangement. But unfortunately, that is not the case. I have continued to live a life undermined and trespassed upon.

I have never had enough time with my daughters. Our time together remains like a trace of exquisite perfume in the wind, beautiful and fleeting.

Having been positioned as the paying babysitter, as the ancillary parent, I get about seventy-three days per year to teach self-care, follow the style kaleidoscope, pack lunches and launder sports uniforms, help two GT[5] young women grow through tough experiences, and, most importantly, equip them for piloting this vast world.

---

5. Gifted & Talented, a special-needs delineation within the school system that applies to children with above-average IQs.

Our heartbeat has become synchronized to the rush of sand whispering through the neck of the hourglass that contains us. No matter how universal their minds' inquiry, or whether we are in the eye of an emotional storm, our borrowed time runs out. I drive them back; proficiently and indiscernibly, we transition. We have come through our tribulations, and they have absolute confidence in my love for them, stored where nobody can touch it. We always hug tightly. And where my influence is halted, I latch onto faith.

Many more questions continue to haunt me. I wonder if, short of walking out on my children, I could have prevented what happened. I have no idea how coparenting will continue to unfold until the kids come of age. And I have still never learned why I was deemed less capable or deserving of caring for our children than my ex-wife.

My ambition, career, earning ability, and worldliness were positioned as divisive in our battle for the girls. I sometimes wonder if they would have been viewed as assets if, rather than a mother, I were a father.

More importantly, I wonder whether a father who expressed the same passion, rage, and confusion I did during those years of hearings would have been commended for his absolute dedication to his children. Would he have overheard people saying, "Wow, this father is not taking no for an answer; he is fighting tooth and nail to fulfill his responsibility to his kids; I wish more were like him"? Doing what I believe any parent had to do, would I have gotten a gold star (maybe even a cookie!) if I were a man?

Sadly, countless fathers have also been alienated from their children, their commitment twisted similarly to mine. However, ambition is still seen through a gender lens, and it is too often cast as a "dirty" word when it refers to women.

Many would like to have been born to a Steve Jobs, or to countless accomplished men before him, because the value of their contributions to the world has not been tainted by their social ineptitude or their deficiency as fathers. Any trauma they might have bestowed on their offspring is justified in society's eyes, because their experiences and work ethic translates into an immensely empowering foundation for the leaders of tomorrow. If you are a mother, however, don't you dare run out of paper towels, miss bedtime, or buy your cookies at Costco.

Our children don't expect us to be perfect. In fact, I bet you their greatest lessons will nest in our faults, our vulnerabilities. So why do we put this pressure on women?

As young women, we are encouraged to soar, to become everything we can—professional athletes, CEOs, and heads of state. But god forbid we shake up motherhood.

The value of motherhood is immeasurable, and I would be the first to fight for the liberation of mothers from centuries of abuse and repression. However, have we gone too far if our legal system cannot keep mothers accountable, even to their children? If we have insulated biological mothers to the point where the only recourse the rest of us have left ourselves, outside absolutely dire circumstances, is to pray that they do the right thing?

Ironically, I am one of the more domestic women you will ever meet. My daughters and I always have dinner together at the table and say grace. I cook, without recipes and rather well; I clean the house for me, not for guests; and I engage with my children deeply about their feelings.

In my story, however, biological motherhood has been so thoroughly weaponized that it should require a license. I bear witness to the fact that the legal system of this great country, sworn to protect the weak, finds itself toothless against a bio-mommy with a nice smile. Women's ability to create life is magical, but don't we discredit the lifelong and selfless work of mothers if we define motherhood disproportionally by this initial act?

And then there is America's original sin: the racial bias. It does appear that America is finally awakening to the racial fault lines within our society. From the Academy Awards to the presidential race, we are recognizing the conditioning that tells us which stories, and whose pain, are worthy of our attention. And, importantly, we are uncomfortably glancing up into the face of our prejudice as we confront how very differently the stories of the previously marginalized are being told.

One of the stark differences is how good parenting is expected to look, and, on the flip side, what the signs of irresponsible parenting are. While tomes have been written crediting all types of cultures with nurturing in children the attributes that help them become healthy adults, some of these cultures get arbitrary preference over others. Most people I came across as I fought for the right to parent my children were not necessarily prejudiced against brown people, but I believe many saw me through the lens of an unconscious bias against brown culture.

Society has a long history of assigning relative magnitude to various sins. Curiously, the sins habitual among those in power tend to be absolved, even as the equal or lesser sins of those without power are deemed to warrant severe punishment. For example, many a hand of the hungry have been chopped off as fair punishment for theft. If we acknowledge that we've been conditioned to agree with the white culture's dread of the raised voice, can we still justify the vilification of a brown mother who raises hers when pushed to do so by injustice?

With all this in mind, I wonder how it might have gone if I had acted more "white," if I had tried harder to blend into the dominant culture of the US family court system. Had I demonstrated greater insecurity with my appearance, projected a need to be liked, suppressed my sexuality, communicated with a tinge of self-belittlement, and opted for passive aggression to get my way, would I have been validated as a truly equal parent?

This is not a dig at white subculture but a challenge to the bias we all may carry—a bias that leads us to unintentionally alienate and punish each other even though we share the mission of raising good kids.

The injustice of our antiquated and biased legal system is further underscored by the growing number and range of alternative families that are raising millions of American children today. Grandparents sacrifice retirement to raise their grandchildren, only to have the biological mother take them away on a whim. In addition to non-biological parents, even committed biological fathers are being sidelined by the system.

Perhaps the path to protecting modern parenting lies through the liberation of women from the shackles of a deeply biased and constraining archetype, and through a celebration of parenthood in its diverse genesis, forms, and colors.

———

Oprah encourages us to keep a list of what we know for sure. Here is my list:

Even if I knew, in every excruciating detail, what would happen, I would do it all again to have my daughters. I would step into that rink and take every hook into my legitimacy as a parent, every jab at my character and every blow to my spirit, and fight to the end for them. While I am sure there are easier ways to raise children, the burn of every tear, the pang of every betrayal, and the finality of my resulting financial woes are all worth it when I look at the two magnificent, exceptional young women I am helping to gear up to inherit this world.

When people show you who they really are, believe them. Many will define themselves by what they take from you. And most are petrified of standing alone, so they will opt to follow the pack. I believe that for most of my life, I saw people for who I *wanted* them to be, and for who they *could* be, even when their own ambition was much more scant.

Only by the grace of god have I managed to stay sober for thirty years. I have not gone crazy. My soul still believes in this world. And my heart, though clad in scar tissue, is still tender and empathetic. I do not hate my ex-wife and wish her no harm. I have not retaliated against her, and I have not thrown her under the bus to our children. So I have not betrayed myself. This hell has not succeeded in obliterating me. I have learned a lot. Standing in my truth, I most often stood alone, but those who still stand by me are worth the thousands who left with the pack. And I treasure my victory: Despite the war waged to keep us apart and regardless of our sparse time together, the love my children and I share is solid and unwavering. No one can ever change that.

We are responsible for our own lives and for the consequences of our choices. No matter what hand we got dealt upon entry into this world, or what has been done to us since, it is our responsibility to find wholeness. When others wrong us, that's on them, and we must find compassion for ourselves in order to heal. But we are the only ones who have the power brand ourselves as victims. And I am not a victim.

Our legal system is deeply antiquated, flawed, and biased and must catch up to the diversity and needs of American families today. Children are the ones who have the most to lose when grown-up drama capriciously redefines who they are supposed to love and for how many days per month, and our social and legal systems have left exposed those who are the most vulnerable. Some laws are moving in the right direction—legalizing same-sex unions, upholding LGBTQ second-parent adoptions, and voting on equal parenting provisions—and the concept of Parental Alienation is also increasingly being acknowledged as another form of domestic violence. But this is not enough. As a society, we must act. And each one of us can help make the first step by changing the conversation around planning for and parenting children from the onset.

To the LGBT community: I am grateful to reengage with you. Frankly, until last year, I couldn't even talk about *And Baby.* What others hailed as a success I could only see as a profound failure; as unfinished business; even as a sadistic twist of fate. The irony of this story coming to you from the very person who put alternative parenting on the map is not lost on me. I have continued to serve the *And Baby* tagline, *Redefining Modern Parenting*, in ways I could have never imagined the day I approved it. I commend all of you who fought for marriage equality. But while we celebrate that victory, we cannot take our eyes off the challenges that remain, including those we face in parenting our children. Even second-parent adoption is not absolute protection. Fortunately, this time many of the solutions lie within, rather than outside, our community, and I am confident that we will continue to succeed if we tackle the injustice the way we always have: head-on.

This book isn't an act of retaliation or a cry for validation. You don't have to like me, agree with how I have handled my situation, or even approve of my publishing this story. But I had to share what happened to my family because nobody else should ever have to go through what we did. I hope that you recognize that we can and *must* do better. The relationship between children and their parents should never be subjected to the whimsy of adult drama and the flighty political deliberations of our society.

So it is with humility that I ask you to join me in a quest to reevaluate our excuses as society for failing to protect children and those who do the vital work of parenting them, regardless of whether they are biologically linked, straight, gay, underage or aging, prepared or knocked up, white or not so much, perfect spouses or fallible ones. Parenting is a privilege, and we owe it to our children to rise to the occasion.

ACKNOWLEDGMENTS

GRACE: favor or goodwill.

To my angels:
I am grateful for all of you. In my darkest days, you have been there for me. Without you, my life would look altogether different.

Nona, for always loving me and never judging me.

Michael, for always believing in me.

Vanessa, for always loving me in spite of me.

Carrie, for always seeing the good in me, especially when I couldn't see it in myself.

My brother, for always helping us, no matter the timeframe or task.

Thomas, for standing by my side and cheering me on, no matter what endeavor or path life had me on.

Judge Baskins, for standing up for the truth and silencing the noise.

Rachael, for not pushing me aside and for making me a priority.

Deborah, for not letting me give up.

Paul, for being a warrior and a protector of the underdog.

Jackson, for being my loyal life raft.

All my friends in NYC, for cheering me on from the sidelines.

Robyn, for all the late-night chats, laughs, and tears we have shared.

Ray, for being like a brother to me.

Gregg, for your unwavering support.

Lori, my forever friend, who has taken the bus with me when the limo wasn't an option.

Amber, for sharing with me through your own struggles, reiterating always that I am a good parent.

Jade, for being there for me always, no matter what.

Marina, for seeing to the core of me.

Jill, for your undeniable support.

Katherine, for helping me honor myself.

My investors, for believing in my talents and creativity.

Rita, for helping make this book possible.

Stephanie, for the support that allowed us to make it through.

Annie, for your ability to craft this story and guide us through the arduous writing process, always supporting our vision.

The girls at BookSparks, for helping get this vital message out.

And for Oprah, my physical-and-non-physical guide: you have been a beaming light throughout my journey, and I am indebted to you.

To my children:
You are my heart. I never really knew love until I had the absolute honor of falling in love with you.

My hope is that through my trials, you will find an inextinguishable source of power within yourselves. There is nothing you cannot achieve. Don't chase happiness; pursue purpose, and happiness will find you. Explore the world. Revel in who you are. Expand but never settle. Stand in your power and stand up for those less fortunate than you. Know and speak your truth, even when it leaves you standing alone. Act as engaged members of a global society. Respect people, the earth, and, most of all yourselves. Give of yourselves generously and empathetically, and you will never run empty.

Honor your responsibility to make this world a better place. Trust that you have the strength, ability, and wisdom to do so. And know that I am by your side, forever, no matter what.

Always.
Mama

To my love:

You have taught me so much about myself. You have showed me that true love feels good—really good—not just some of the time but most of the time, and that when two souls venture down a journey together it is just that: a journey. We have climbed mountains, crossed over rivers, and run through meadows. You make me laugh and sometimes cry, but most of all you bring joy and happiness to my life. I am forever grateful for what we have and what we have learned. I will cherish you for all my days forward. The journey continues . . .

ABOUT THE AUTHOR

MICHELLE DARNÉ has been a prominent figure in the fashion, advertising, marketing, publishing, and entertainment industries for more than thirty years. In 2000, she bet on a market nobody believed existed when she decided to publish *And Baby Magazine: Redefining Modern Parenting,* which became the pioneer national magazine to focus on alternative parenting. Within a few years, *And Baby* became a radio show with 7 million listeners, and then a TV series followed by 35 million homes through Time Warner cable. In 2005, the National Gay & Lesbian Chamber of Commerce (NGLCC) named Darné the inaugural Entrepreneur of the Year. She is currently the CEO and executive producer of Patina Entertainment, a digital media company providing quality content for underserved niche markets. To amplify the impact she aims to have through *Parent Deleted,* she also recently founded Simply Parent, a non-profit that is dedicated to forging a society where good parenting is protected in all its diverse geneses, forms, and colors.

SELECTED TITLES FROM
SHE WRITES PRESS

She Writes Press is an independent publishing company founded to serve women writers everywhere. Visit us at www.shewritespress.com.

Pieces of Me: Rescuing My Kidnapped Daughters by Lizbeth Meredith. 978-1-63152-834-7. When her daughters are kidnapped and taken to Greece by their non-custodial father, single mom Lizbeth Meredith vows to bring them home—and give them a better childhood than her own.

Loveyoubye: Holding Fast, Letting Go, and Then There's the Dog by Rossandra White. $16.95, 978-1-938314-50-6. A soul-searching memoir detailing the painful, but ultimately liberating, disintegration of a twenty-five-year marriage.

Stepmother: A Memoir by Marianne Lile. $16.95, 978-1-63152-089-1. Lile describes the complexities of the stepmom position, in a family and in the community, and shares her experience wearing a tag that is often misunderstood and weighed down by the numerous myths in society.

Breathe: A Memoir of Motherhood, Grief, and Family Conflict by Kelly Kittel. $16.95, 978-1-938314-78-0. A mother's heartbreaking account of losing two sons in the span of nine months—and learning, despite all the obstacles in her way, to find joy in life again.

Fire Season: A Memoir by Hollye Dexter. $16.95, 978-1-63152-974-0. After she loses everything in a fire, Hollye Dexter's life spirals downward and she begins to unravel—but when she finds herself at the brink of losing her husband, she is forced to dig within herself for the strength to keep her family together.

Falling Together: How to Find Balance, Joy, and Meaningful Change When Your Life Seems to be Falling Apart by Donna Cardillo. $16.95, 978-1-63152-077-8. A funny, big-hearted self-help memoir that tackles divorce, caregiving, burnout, major illness, fears, and low self-esteem—and explores the renewal that comes when we are able to meet these challenges with courage.